## PREVENT, SURVIVE, AND RECOVER
## WITH THE FACTS

175,000 people will die from strokes this year. Some of them do not have to. A variety of new medical and preventive procedures can cut down the risk of having a serious stroke. And stroke victims can be helped to restore their independence and self-esteem with advanced rehabilitative approaches that utilize trained teams of medical professionals and newly developed therapies. But it's your responsibility to know the facts to fight back against the third leading killer in America. Find out:

- What's the single most important factor that increases your risk of stroke?
- What's the role of weight, cholesterol, and oral contraceptives?
- How are aging and strokes related?
- How can ignoring warning signs kill you?
- Who has recovered from a serious stroke—and how?
- What are the steps to returning to a full, productive life?

**THE STROKE FACT BOOK**

## QUANTITY PURCHASES

# THE
# STROKE
# FACT BOOK

## Conn Foley, M.D.
## and
## H. F. Pizer, PA-C

BANTAM BOOKS
TORONTO • NEW YORK • LONDON • SYDNEY • AUCKLAND

To Mom and Dad who have made everything possible.
To Carmel Aisling and Sinbar who make all worthwhile.

*This book is not intended to replace
your own physician with whom you should
consult before taking any medication or
considering treatment.*

THE STROKE FACT BOOK
*A Bantam Book / June 1985*

ISBN 0-553-24961-4

*Published simultaneously in the United States and Canada*

*Bantam Books are published by Bantam Books, Inc. Its trade-
mark, consisting of the words "Bantam Books" and the por-
trayal of a rooster, is Registered in U.S. Patent and Trademark
Office and in other countries. Marca Registrada. Bantam
Books, Inc., 666 Fifth Avenue, New York, New York 10103.*

PRINTED IN THE UNITED STATES OF AMERICA

O      0 9 8 7 6 5 4 3 2 1

# Acknowledgments

We would like to thank the staff of the Jewish Institute for Geriatric Care in New Hyde Park, New York, who participated in the writing and editing of this book.

Charluta Badlani, M.D.—Chief of Geriatric Rehabilitation
Donna Kass, R.P.T.—Coordinator of Physical Medicine and Rehabilitation
Joan Goldberger, S.T.—Speech Therapist
Herbert Hildebrandt, M.S.W.—Assistant Director of Social Work
Marion Goldstein, M.S.W.—Director of Social Work
Kenneth Kahaner, M.D.—Chief of Geriatric Psychiatry
Nerlige Basavaraju, M.D.—Attending Physician/Geriatric Neurologist
Giselle Wolf-Klein, M.D.—Attending Physician/Physician-in-Charge of Geriatric Community Health Center
David Orchanian, O.T.—Senior Occupational Therapist
Betty Joblove, O.T.—Chief of Occupational Therapy
Stewart Scharfman, R.P.T.—Supervisor of Physical Therapy
Eleanor Krause—Medical Secretary
Lorraine Oppedisano—Medical Secretary
Evelyn Massett, R.N.—Rehabilitation Clinician
Felix Silverstone, M.D.—Associate Medical Director
Saul Kamen, D.D.S.—Chief of Geriatric Dentistry
Pamela Hoffman, M.D.—Physician-in-Charge of Geriatric Medical Education
Harry Smith, M.S.—Director of Pharmacy
Myra Peskowitz, R.N.—Director of Nursing
David Glaser—Chief Executive Officer

# Contents

# THE
# STROKE
# FACT BOOK

# 1

# Some Important Facts About Strokes

Strokes have been afflicting mankind since Creation. By studying the remains of mummies we know that the ancient Egyptians had strokes. The writings of Hippocrates, the father of Western medicine, indicate that the Greeks also suffered from *apoplexia*, the term they used to describe a sudden, astonishing shock to the senses—a concept that aptly describes a stroke attack today.

Since the time of the ancients, we have acquired a fairly sound understanding of why most strokes occur. With this knowledge we can develop strategies for preventing their onset. Moreover, should a stroke occur, there are new and increasingly effective methods for restoring bodily functions and improving mental outlook.

Strokes are, nevertheless, the third leading cause of death in modern, industrialized nations. At least 500,000 individuals suffer an episode each year in the United States. About 2½ million survive, and with intensive rehabilitation, many can lead active lives.

The point is that even if a stroke strikes, it is possible to survive and recover. Louis Pasteur, the French scientist, suffered a stroke and yet lived another 24 years and subsequently developed the principles of vaccination against disease. Sir Winston Churchill also was the victim of this disease and, despite his affliction, lived to regain the prime ministry of

Great Britain. Presidents Dwight Eisenhower and Franklin Delano Roosevelt, actress Patricia Neal, dancer and choreographer Agnes DeMille, and Chairman Mao Tse-tung had strokes and nevertheless continued to lead active lives. Having a stroke does not mean that one should give up hope or resign oneself to a life of disability and social withdrawal.

## What Is a Stroke?

Despite the fact that stroke is relatively common, few lay people seem to be knowledgeable about its underlying causes, the way in which it produces disability, or how it can be treated and prevented. This may be due to the fact that other illnesses like cancer, heart disease, arthritis, and diabetes have received more public attention in recent years. But, because stroke is a common problem, and one that can be prevented as well as treated, it is important that we learn about it.

The medical term for a stroke is a *cerebrovascular accident*, often abbreviated as a *CVA*. It is an injury to the nervous system that occurs when adequate supply of oxygen and nutrients fails to reach portions of the brain. In most cases this injury is not the result of a blow to the head. Instead, it arises as a spontaneous event; usually due to a long-standing degeneration of the body's blood vessels. Less commonly, a CVA may occur because of an inborn abnormality or weakness of the brain's vasculature.

Most cerebrovascular accidents are caused by blood clots that impair the blood flow and produce irreversible injury to brain cells. When this occurs in the brain it is called a *cerebral infarction* and is analagous to the more commonly understood heart attack or *myocardial infarction*.

The symptoms of paralysis, impaired sensation, and difficulties in seeing or communicating that we associate with a stroke are the direct result of this process. The diseases of the circulatory system that predispose individuals to heart attacks are also at work in producing strokes. This process and the symptoms of a stroke that result are discussed more fully in chapters 2–4.

The most common type of stroke, which occurs in 30–45 percent of cases, is caused by a blood clot that forms in one of the arteries of the brain. The medical term for this is a *thrombus*, and the process is *cerebral thrombosis*. Like heart attacks, thrombosis occurs most frequently in blood vessels that have already been damaged by *atherosclerosis* (hardening of the arteries).

In about 20–33 percent of all strokes, a blood clot will form in the heart or in one of the blood vessels of the neck or chest, and travel into the brain. This clot *(embolus)* migrates downstream (away from the heart) in the ever-narrowing vascular network. Eventually it will be too large to pass through and will cause an obstruction of normal blood flow. The overall effect is similar to that of cerebral thrombosis and may be called a *cerebral embolism*. This can also occur in other parts of the body. In the lungs, for instance, it is called *pulmonary embolism*. In the brain and the lungs, tissues downstream to the thrombus or embolus are deprived of vital oxygen and nutrients and undergo permanent injury.

In a relatively small number of cases—perhaps only 5–15 percent—a cerebrovascular accident results from *hemorrhage* within the brain (rupture of a blood vessel). We are all familiar with slang expressions like, "Don't get upset, you'll burst a blood vessel," or, "Don't strain yourself, you'll have a hemorrhage." These statements refer to *cerebral hemorrhage*. Most cases of cerebral hemorrhage are not related to anxiety, but occur in the face of the long-standing degenerative effects of high blood pressure, atherosclerosis, and other conditions that weaken the cerebral blood vessels. Figure 1 illustrates the causes of strokes. More facts about this subject will be presented in chapter 2.

## The Age Factor

The majority of strokes occur in the seventh decade of life and it is rare for anyone under the age of thirty-five to have a CVA. Interestingly, it appears that the overall frequency of strokes in developing nations is rising, possibly because of the increased longevity of the population. What, then, is the relationship between strokes and the aging process?

Most medical scientists do not accept the concept that CVAs are an inevitable outcome of aging. They feel, instead, that these episodes are the result of degenerative and chronic

**Figure 1**

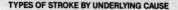

TYPES OF STROKE BY UNDERLYING CAUSE

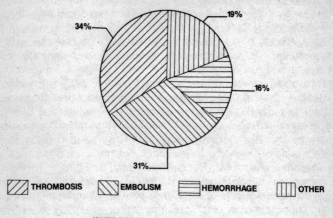

ADAPTED FROM DATA COMPILED BY MOHR, JP ET. AL
HARVARD COOPERATIVE STROKE REGISTRY, 1978

disorders like *hypertension* (high blood pressure), diabetes, amd atherosclerosis that affect the heart and blood vessels. Tobacco smoking, the use of birth control pills, and certain other life-style practices are also likely to be relevant (see chapter 4). It appears that the accumulated effect of these pathological processes is not apparent until later in life when the degenerative effects have been at work for many years. It would be wrong to consider these conditions or strokes, in general, as a normal result of aging.

## Preventing Strokes

Understanding that strokes are the product of identifiable degenerative processes allows us to develop strategies for its prevention. Altering life-style practices, instituting basic preventive health measures (like controlling blood pressure) and becoming aware of possible warning signs of a stroke are the principles of a CVA prevention program. What is also satisfying about this approach is that these measures can be beneficial in preventing other common medical problems like heart disease, diabetes, and possibly cancer.

A hopeful sign is that over the last thirty years the overall death rate and frequency of cerebrovascular accidents has declined slightly in the United States. This is somewhat surprising since the death rate due to heart attacks has been relatively stable. It may be that we are learning to control hypertension and to modify our life-styles in positive directions. But more needs to be accomplished, since strokes are still our number three killer.

Some people worry about the risk of having a second stroke episode after recovering from their first one. It appears that there are preventive measures that can reduce this risk. In Rochester, Minnesota, efforts by the Mayo Clinic appear to have been beneficial in this regard. This is yet another sign that points to the importance of preventive measures (see chapter 4).

Many of the life-style changes like dietary modification, participation in a regular exercise program, and the elimination of smoking, are stroke prevention strategies that should be implemented long before individuals reach their seventies. Remember that the process of vascular degeneration that predisposes an individual to strokes occurs over many years. We advise those who may feel that they are too young to worry about strokes to read about its prevention now. The efforts that are made today are likely to be helpful in later years.

## Stroke Rehabilitation

The modern stroke rehabilitation program requires the coordinated efforts of many health practitioners: physicians, nurses, and counselors; and physical, occupational, and speech therapists. Involved family members and other stroke victims can also make positive impact on the recovery process. Unfortunately, many stroke victims are not given the benefit of a modern, comprehensive stroke rehabilitation program.

Chapters 6–10 describe the services required for optimal stroke rehabilitation. We favor the organization of these activities in a *stroke unit*. Our experience at the Jewish Institute for Geriatric Care in New Hyde Park, New York, and the experience of other institutions worldwide, favors this concept as well.

We suggest that patients and families learn about the stroke unit and become knowledgeable about the many professionals associated with it. If you do not feel that you are receiving the full range of needed services, or that they are not being delivered in a coordinated and caring fashion, it may be helpful to seek out a stroke unit. We believe that everyone who suffers a cerebrovascular accident deserves an optimal effort at rehabilitation.

# The Cost of Stroke Rehabilitation

Most individuals who suffer a stroke require rehabilitation and supportive care. Approximately 40 percent of those who survive a CVA will have only mild residual impairment and continue to lead independent lives. Another 40 percent will need some type of daily supportive care on a long-term basis, and 10 percent will require long-term institutionalization. Individuals in all three groups will require varying degrees of medical, social, and supportive services after their discharge from the hospital or rehabilitation facility.

The cost of this care is enormous for both the individual and society. A typical nursing home bill is likely to exceed $20,000 on a yearly basis. The total cost of caring for all persons who have strokes runs into billions annually. What is more important, perhaps, is the cost in terms of lost human capacity and suffering.

# Coping with a Stroke

The suddenness of a CVA inevitably catches victim, family, and friends off guard. As you shall see from the many stories included in this book, individuals are quickly swept from productive occupations, family responsibilities, and social activity and placed in a dependent situation.

It is not surprising that almost everyone who is affected by a stroke finds the job of coping to be a difficult one. For most people the task requires the help of trained professionals: a psychiatrist, a psychologist, a social worker, a knowledgeable physician, and trained nurses. The rehabilitative efforts provided by speech, occupational, and physical therapy also contribute to successful adaptation to the stress of the stroke illness.

There is a common tendency on the part of the stroke patient and his family to develop a pessimistic, sad, often depressed attitude. These feelings act to stymie the rehabilitative work. As progress in regaining function is further impaired, added negative emotions arise and a vicious circle is created.

This is another reason why stroke units appear to be the best structure for carrying out the rehabilitation process, since staff members are trained to cope with the emotional and spiritual needs of the patient and family. The work toward regaining function is further aided by the support and encouragement that comes from others who are involved in the recovery process.

Chapters 9 and 10 deal with the psychological problems that arise in the aftermath of a stroke and strategies for overcoming them. The important point to remember is that anyone who has suffered a stroke, and all those who are close to that person, should have the benefit of knowledgeable professionals who can help the person cope with negative emotions. No one should attempt to deal with the depression, anxiety, anger, denial, and frustration caused by a stroke alone.

## To Review

1. Mankind has been afflicted by strokes since the beginning of history. Our knowledge has improved, so that now much can be done to prevent strokes and to provide rehabilitation for its sufferers.

2. The medical terminology for a stroke is a *cerebrovascular accident,* or a *CVA.* It is an injury sustained to the brain's cells when the blood supply is impaired; strokes are usually the result of long-term degenerative processes in the body's blood vessels.

3. When a clot forms in an artery and obstructs blood flow, it is called a thrombus; if the clot forms in one area of the body and migrates to another, it is called an embolus; the rupture of a blood vessel is called a hemorrhage, all of which can cause a cerebrovascular accident.

4. A stroke is *not* the normal result of aging. Factors like hypertension, diabetes, and atherosclerosis that affect the body's blood vessels, create an increased risk for strokes. Controlling these risk factors can reduce the likelihood of suffering a CVA.

5. Many life-style factors like tobacco smoking, dietary indiscretion, lack of exercise, and obesity, appear to contribute to the risk of having a stroke. Controlling such life-style factors may be more significant for preventing strokes than specific interventions devised by one's physician. In any event, a stroke prevention program that combines personal changes in life-style and appropriate medical services is also helpful for reducing the risk of suffering other illnesses common to modern society (see chapter 4).

6. The stroke unit is a coordinated team approach that is thought to be the most effective way to provide essential rehabilitation services while reducing the cost of strokes, both in terms of lost human capacity and health care dollars (see chapters 6–8).

7. Virtually every stroke victim and their close family members can expect to undergo severe emotional distress. Effective counseling and psychological therapy is an essential part of the stroke rehabilitation effort (see chapter 9). There are numerous services and financial programs that help both individuals and families cope with the social and monetary issues (see chapter 10).

# 2

# The Nervous System Reacts to a Stroke

The human brain is composed of different, highly specialized regions that work in concert. Its segmental nature is the result of millions of years of evolution in which more developed and specialized regions gradually took over to regulate our needs. Lower (inferior) portions control respiration, hunger, pain, and other basic functions. Areas located on the surface of the brain *(cortex)* control more complex activities like logical thought.

The system is so highly specialized that the region for appreciating and remembering music, for instance, is different from that for speech. And, the area for seeing and understanding a sporting event on television is different from that for reading a newspaper. The selective impairment that occurs after a stroke is the result of injury to one or more of these highly differentiated regions.

The actual damage inflicted by a CVA in any individual is dependent on two factors: the specific site of the cerebral injury, and the amount of cerebral tissue that is damaged. Unfortunately, brain cells do not regenerate. The brain is not like bones, skin, and the stomach lining, for instance, which have the capability of replacing damaged tissue with normal cells. Nevertheless, we do recoup cerebral losses by retraining the cells that have been left undamaged, possibly by activating underused or new neurological pathways. This is the basis upon which rehabilitative efforts work (see chapters 6–8).

# Thrombosis and Embolism

The majority of strokes occur because the arteries of the body, particularly those supplying blood to the brain, undergo a gradual degenerative process, called atherosclerosis (see chapter 1). It is a pathological process and not a normal aspect of human aging. Commonly, it is called hardening of the arteries and may be seen in the heart, kidney, and blood vessels located in other parts of the body.

Atherosclerosis appears as rough, irregular fatty deposits that collect in the inner lining of the arteries. It may be identified by the time certain individuals reach their early twenties and continues in the face of advancing years (and possibly dietary indiscretion) until it may produce symptoms later on in life. This information has been gathered from studying autopsies of young persons who die in automobile accidents or during wartime. Fortunately, the body's blood vessels have a significant reserve capacity. In general, manifestations of atherosclerosis, particularly reduced blood flow, do not occur until the vessel is two thirds blocked.

To understand the process of producing hardened, rough, and irregular areas of fatty deposit, called *atheromas,* imagine a garden hose that has been allowed to collect dirt, mineral deposits, and debris. The more the inner lining of the hose becomes speckled with these deposits, the more difficult it will be for water to flow through it. The effect of reducing the flow of water will be to further increase the collection of dirt and minerals inside the hose. The process will likely continue until the hose becomes completely clogged, or until it bursts from the increased pressure.

In the human body, this disease process continues until a blood clot, or *thrombosis,* forms, ultimately clogging all, or a major portion of, the blood vessel. A thrombus is also likely to form in areas where blood vessels turn, divide, or kink. In an area where a small thrombus has formed, there is a tendency for the clot to enlarge. Then, as blood flow slows, clot-forming elements are deposited producing an enlarging or *propagating thrombus.*

High blood pressure has an aggravating effect on athero-sclerosis by driving the hardened deposits into the lining of the arterial wall. This further fixes the atheroma into the artery and reduces its resiliency, as it did in our garden hose example. Over the years this process will further increase blood pressure and aggravate atherosclerosis. It is, therefore, not surprising that most strokes occur in the face of advanced atherosclerosis and high blood pressure.

The body's arterial system is like a tree. It is made up of large trunks of arteries and ever-narrowing branches of blood vessels. *Emboli* are blood clots that form in a diseased artery or the heart and move downstream, away from the heart. They pass through the arterial vasculature, until they lodge in the progressively narrowing system.

Approximately thirty to thirty-five percent of strokes appear to be the result of this process: a clot forms in an area already damaged by atherosclerosis, breaks loose and moves downstream until it can pass no further. Typical sites of embolus formation are diseased heart valves or the *carotid arteries,* the principal arterial vessels in the neck.

Emboli do not necessarily travel only to the brain, but may also produce disease in the legs, lungs, kidneys, and intestine. High blood pressure, by the way, appears to be a factor in the genesis of emboli, as well as thrombi.

## How a Stroke Inflicts Damage

All strokes result from restriction of blood flow to the nerve cells of the brain. These cells *(neurons)* require a constant flow of oxygen and nutrients supplied by the bloodstream. Any decrease in this flow can produce irreversible injury to the sensitive nerve cells that control higher order human functioning.

Recent studies with laboratory animals have shown that the degree of injury to cerebral cells is dependent on the amount of restriction of blood flow and the duration of time that restriction lasts. In rats, for instance, 10 minutes of complete deprivation of cerebral circulation will produce cell death. In cats, 5–8 minutes of circulatory failure is needed to produce a similar result. In humans, it appears that 5–10 minutes of complete *occlusion* (obstruction) to an area of the brain is required. The same process also occurs in coronary arteries, producing a heart attack *(myocardial infarction);* or happen in the legs to create *gangrene* and tissue death.

In real life, however, people may not suffer *complete* occlusion of a cerebral vessel and still suffer a stroke. This is, perhaps, why some cerebrovascular accidents develop slowly over hours or even days.

Recent work with laboratory animals has demonstrated that even a partial impairment of cerebral flow, if allowed to continue for a sufficient period of time, may produce irreversible brain injury. Since some strokes may be the result of diminished, but not completely interrupted cerebral circulation over an *extended* period, scientists are working toward future medical advances to limit the damage inflicted in these situations.

The actual physiological events produced during a stroke have come under intensive scrutiny in recent years. It appears that once blood flow to cerebral neurons diminishes, a series of characteristic steps occur. At first the membrane that surrounds each affected brain cell becomes "leaky," spilling its contents of potassium (a salty mineral needed for producing electrical impulses) and *ATP (adenosine triphosphate,* an energy-producing biochemical found naturally in the body). Fluid quickly accumulates in the spaces between the blood vessel and the neuron.

As fluid engorges the space between cells and blood vessels, it becomes increasingly difficult for oxygen and nutrients to pass from the bloodstream into the damaged neuron. This initial injury produces a vicious circle in which more cellular injury results. Unless oxygen and nutrients can cross from the bloodstream to the cells, irreversible cell death will occur.

In Figure 2, we can see a schematic representation of what some scientists think may go on in the general area of impaired blood flow. Nerve cells immediately downstream to the halted circulation are likely to die within a few minutes (or in a slightly longer period of time, if blood flow is only partially interrupted). These dead cells form a zone of *infarction.* This is dead tissue that will not regenerate.

Further downstream is a zone of injury *(penumbra).* This area may be supplied by alternative blood vessels *(collaterals).*

**Figure 2**

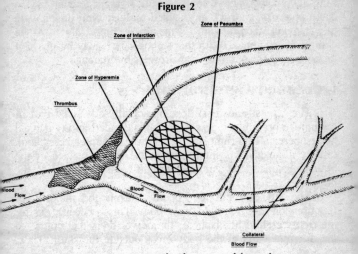

This region, now compromised, may ultimately return to normal functioning.

A third area, that of *hyperemia,* may also exist. Here the blood vessels are congested and swollen, and may also have potential for recovery. It is not completely understood why the two regions of hyperemia and penumbra exist, because they are reacting quite differently to the stroke process. This effect, however, may serve to minimize the total area of infarction that results.

The presence of these two zones, however, poses potential problems for medical scientists. The array of treatments that currently exist for intervening in the stroke process, are often not beneficial to both zones at the same time. Raising blood pressure, for instance (which may help if the heart is injured or not pumping properly), will likely improve conditions in the penumbral region, but further congest the zone of hyperemia. Lowering blood pressure, on the other hand, may relieve the area of hyperemia, but reduce blood flow in the already compromised penumbra.

Other strategies, such as altering blood levels of *glucose* (an energy-producing biochemical found naturally in the body) and oxygen, also regulate blood flow within the brain but do not benefit both hyperemic and penumbral regions at the same time. New approaches to the medical management of the acute phase of a stroke are needed to selectively manipulate the relevant factors and to maximize blood flow to the compromised zones. With this technology it may be possible to save cerebral neurons from irreversible damage.

# Left-Sided Cerebral Injuries

The largest and most developmentally advanced part of the human brain is the *cerebrum* that is divided into two equal hemispheres. The right and left cerebral hemispheres look exactly alike and constitute almost the entire surface of the brain substance, but control very different functions of the body.

The left cerebral hemisphere controls the majority of functions on the *right side of the body*. This is because, as for the right cerebral hemisphere, the nerve fibers that course to the different parts of the body cross outside the skull. Thus,

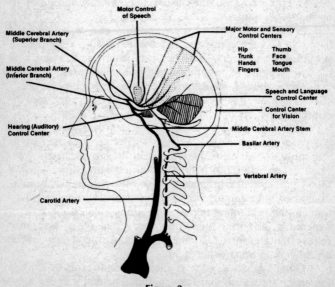

**Figure 3**
**Left Cerebral Hemisphere**
**Major Blood Vessels and Areas of Functional Control**

left-sided brain injury produces right-sided sensory and motor deficit and vice versus. Figure 3 is a schematic representation of the left cerebral hemisphere.

The following story is an example of a left cerebral injury. Because of the speech and language deficit that resulted, the story is told by a friend.

I have known Martha to be an active mother, teacher, friend, and community volunteer for thirty years. She was seventy-three when she had the stroke, but she never seemed to be a sickly person. We were all terribly shocked when it happened. It was as though she was with us one day and then gone the next. It wasn't as though she died, or remained unconscious, but she changed in many ways.

If Martha had a vice, it was her love for sweets: cookies, candy, and cakes. We were baking Christmas cookies together and it was early December. We had been baking cookies for our respective families together for many years. We would work in the kitchen and talk. As the cookies were finished we would freeze the treats until our families united for the holidays. It was a kind of ritual for us.

We were talking away when all of a sudden Martha turned quite ashen. She had to hold herself up by leaning on the kitchen counter. I went over and asked her what was wrong, but she couldn't say a single word. She just stared at me, breathing kind of funny, like she was trying to catch her breath.

I was terrified. I thought that she might be having a heart attack or maybe a stroke. I pulled a chair under her. Her legs buckled, just as I got the chair to her, and she slumped over. The right side of her face seemed to sag and she was drooling from the side of her mouth. Also, her right arm lay next to her body and she couldn't seem to move it.

I called the hospital and they sent an ambulance. It was terrifying how quickly things happened. Most of all, it was terrible that she couldn't speak and tell me what was wrong.

This case history demonstrates that the nerve centers located in the cerebral hemispheres control a variety of *motor* and *sensory* functions. These include muscular activities that produce movement and the sensations of touch, temperature, pain, and position. In addition, they regulate other *conscious* activities like the voluntary control of bowel and bladder elimination, vision, hearing, and speech.

Figure 3 is a schematic representation of the geography of these areas of functional control.

As was previously mentioned, a stroke is the result of an injury to one or more of the brain's blood vessels. In this case, the vascular insult occurred in the distribution of the *middle cerebral artery (MCA)*, the largest of the cerebral vessels.

The MCA is connected to the heart by the carotid artery. Thus, impairment of blood flow to areas supplied by the MCA may be due to an abnormality of the carotid artery or middle cerebral artery. Circulation also may be interrupted by an embolus that forms in the heart or carotid artery and that moves downstream and lodges in the MCA. In the case history just described, the stroke may have been the result of occlusion of the MCA or the left carotid artery of the neck.

A cerebrovascular accident in the region of the middle cerebral artery in the left cerebral hemisphere may—

1. produce loss of muscular movement and coordination of the *right* side of the face, trunk, arm, and leg;
2. impair sensory appreciation of heat, cold, pain, and position on the *right* side;
3. create a variety of language deficits *(aphasia)*: difficulty speaking or understanding speech, writing, reading, and understanding gestures;
4. produce uncoordinated movements of the lips, mouth, tongue, and vocal cords that also may impair speech *(dysarthria)*;
5. create blind spots in the visual field, usually on the right side;
6. produce a slow and cautious personality;
7. produce memory gaps for recent and/or past events.

The left cerebral hemisphere is unique in that it controls language function in virtually all right-handed persons and in approximately fifty percent of individuals who are left-handed. In a small number, neither left nor right cerebral hemisphere is dominant. Rather than being a blessing, it often afflicts these individuals with a variety of speech and language problems. Evidently it is helpful to have one cerebral hemisphere dominant with regard to linguistic activities.

The ability to communicate through speaking, using gestures, writing, reading, and understanding language is, perhaps, the most complex and advanced of human abilities.

There are many types of language deficits (aphasias). Some people, for example, can speak, but have an impairment in their understanding of what is said to them. Other individuals may speak individual words properly, but the meaning of their communication is garbled. Others stammer; while they know what they wish to say, they cannot seem to get the words out properly.

Interestingly, the breakdown of language function is more complex than previously thought by medical scientists. For most people the right side of the brain controls memory, awareness, and appreciation of music. Thus, an individual who suffers a left-sided cerebrovascular accident may be totally unable to speak, but may sing the correct words if given a musical cue. There are many types of aphasia (see chapter 8).

# Right-Sided Cerebral Injuries

The right side of the brain controls the majority of functions on the left side of the body. Damage produced by strokes of the right cerebral hemisphere may also create a rather strange impairment of spatial sensation. Often people with this injury will attempt to move rapidly, commonly making errors in judgment. Other individuals will totally ignore the existence of one or more parts of their body. One patient comes to mind, because he would forget about his left hand while eating and leave it on his plate. It caused him great frustration that he could not scoop his own hand onto his fork and eat it as part of his meal.

The following story is an example of a cerebrovascular accident affecting the *right cerebral hemisphere:*

> Except for some high blood pressure treated by my doctor, at age sixty-three I rarely had time or interest for thinking about my health. I was a go-getter type of person, never thinking about retirement or slowing up in any way.
>
> On August 27—I distinctly remember the date—I felt that something was wrong the moment I got up in the morning. I reached for the alarm clock that sits by the bed and couldn't find the little button for turning on the "sleep and snooze." I was so clumsy that I knocked over the lamp that sits on the bed table.
>
> When I tried to get up my legs were weak, I was dizzy, and I felt a little sick to my stomach. It was as though I was drunk. I wobbled to the kitchen and had an awful lot of difficulty trying to stand without holding on to the countertop. It took all my concentration to put water on for coffee and my vision was blurred. I felt like there was a heavy weight on my shoulders and my mind was not clear.
>
> I stumbled through the living room, bumped into the furniture (even though it hadn't changed place in years), and lost my balance bending over for the paper. I didn't have a single defined pain, but my body ached. I felt like I was observing an illness in someone else, but I was frightened—very frightened—that I was having a stroke, or a tumor, or maybe having some strange kind of epileptic seizure.
>
> I tried calling my doctor, but I couldn't remember his number or find it in my phone book. I had difficulty mouthing my words, even though I knew what I wanted to say when the information operator came on the line. The numbers I wrote down didn't sit straight on the paper. But somehow I was able to reach his office.
>
> He called an ambulance for me and they brought me to the hospital. I think that he knew over the

phone that I was having a stroke, or that maybe I had had a stroke during the night. It was the strangest feeling. I wasn't in pain, but things were definitely not right. I felt exhausted and confused. I had weakness in my left arm and leg, and lots of pins and needles. I was worried that I was having a heart attack, but my chest was not painful. I think that I passed out when we were talking on the telephone, because I don't remember anything about the ride to the hospital.

Injury to the middle cerebral artery of the *right* cerebral hemisphere, like the episode just described, may produce one or more of the following deficits:

1. Weakness *(hemiparesis)*, or paralysis *(hemiplegia)*, or lack of coordination of the face, trunk, arm, and leg on the *left* side of the body
2. Numbness, tingling, impairment of touch, pain, temperature, and position sense *(dysesthesia)* on the *left* side of the body
3. Impaired awareness of spatial relationships, including poor perception of distance *(dysmetria)*
4. Poor understanding or awareness about the position of limbs and other body parts in space, usually on the *left* side
5. Denial of the existence of a part of the body, usually on the *left* side *(anosagnosia)*
6. Difficulty dressing appropriately, particularly for the *left* side *(dressing apraxia)*
7. Visual misperceptions; complete loss of recognition on the *left* side of the visual field *(hemianopia)*
8. Impulsive behavior, quick movements, imprecise movement, and errors of judgment

Both right and left middle cerebral arteries have many branches. The major ones are shown in Figure 3, p. 14. The largest, or *superior* trunk, controls motor and sensory functions that are commonly affected by a stroke. In the CVA just described, there was a disruption of blood flow to a zone supplied by the superior portion of the MCA. This accounts for the numbness and weakness of the left arm and leg. While he was basically unaware of it, he also had difficulty appreciating objects on his left side. This explains the fact that he bumped into the furniture on his way to get the morning paper. And, while he was also somewhat unaware of it, he may have had some loss in his left visual field, which contributed to his difficulty writing down the physician's telephone number.

Impairment of blood flow in the middle cerebral artery may also produce areas of blindness in the normal visual field. A common problem is *homonymous hemianopia* where both the nasal side of vision in one eye and the temporal side of the other eye's vision is lost to view. If, for instance, you are standing to the left side of someone with a left homonymous hemianopia, you are likely to be in an area that cannot be perceived. In general, it is extremely important for family and friends to be aware of this problem and to position themselves well within the normal area of vision.

Another point is that the inability to speak intelligible words can be due to the immediate shock of the stroke and its disruptive effects on the muscles that coordinate speech. This produces difficulty in articulating words and slurred or otherwise difficult-to-understand speech. This is different from expressive language disorders that usually occur in left cerebral injuries.

A final point is that most strokes seem to produce a period of weakness, fatigue, and confusion. This appears to be a generalized physiological reaction to a CVA. It is likely that the person in the last example woke up in the hospital with a sense of fatigue as well as some confusion and disorientation. It is, thus, not surprising that strokes are often referred to as a shock by the nonmedical public. It is, in truth, a sudden shock to the senses.

## Lacunar Strokes

The *lacunar stroke* was first described by the French physician, Pierre Marie, at the beginning of the twentieth century. He noted that some individuals appeared to suffer small strokes that left few serious permanent deficits. It is now thought that about fifteen to twenty percent of all cerebrovascular accidents come under this category.

The following is an example of a lacunar stroke related by the patient himself. Since the episode he has been able to continue living a productive and active life-style, taking some stroke prevention precautions (see chapter 4).

> I felt completely well before I had my stroke and never thought of myself as a sick person. When one day I woke up with a weakness on my left side I was surprised, but not really alarmed. I thought that perhaps I had slept in an awkward position.
>
> But I was incredibly clumsy when I tried to use my hand and I had a lot of difficulty walking. I was awkward, I guess; clumsy as though a bit drunk. But I hadn't had any alcohol whatsoever.
>
> I still felt rather well. I was confused, but not because my brain wasn't working properly. It was mostly because I didn't have an explanation for the fact that my balance and coordination was off. My head felt fine, my eyes could see straight, but why couldn't I walk straight and stand up without getting dizzy. It just didn't make any sense at all.

Lacunar strokes, such as this one, occur when very small arteries within the brain become blocked. The cells downstream to the area of the occlusion die, but since the total area of injury is small, only minor deficits may result. Within a few months of the death of these cerebral cells a very small cavity (*lacune* in French) is produced.

Lacunar strokes usually occur in the face of fairly advanced atherosclerosis and hypertension. Generally there are at least four small, patchy lacunes produced by a single cerebrovascular accident. These defects may occur over a relatively large area of the brain or be localized.

The symptoms of a lacunar stroke may develop over hours or days. Commonly they produce only *motor* deficits such as weakness and/or poor coordination. It is possible, however, to have purely sensory loss and a combination of motor and sensory deficits.

Speech and language ability is usually preserved in a lacunar stroke. However, it may be difficult to utter words due to partial paralysis of the lips, tongue, mouth, or vocal cords. Fortunately, lacunar strokes usually leave *mentation* (mental activity) and personality intact.

## Other Areas of Cerebral Injuries

Not all strokes affect the area of the brain supplied by the middle cerebral artery or involve small patchy areas like the lacunar stroke. The rear (posterior) portion of the brain is supplied by blood from the posterior cerebral and vertebro-basilar arteries. The front and interior of the brain substance (anterior and medial regions, respectively) receive blood via the anterior cerebral artery. Occlusion of any of these vessels may produce a variety of symptoms and deficits.

The *anterior cerebral artery* carries blood to the front and middle portions of the brain and to a variety of important structures that lie deep within the hemispheres. Symptoms of anterior cerebral artery stroke include—

1. paralysis of the leg, usually more severe than in the arm, on the side opposite to the occluded vessel;
2. loss of sensation in the opposite toes, foot, and leg;
3. loss of conscious control over bowel and/or bladder function;
4. difficulty with balance;
5. lack of spontaneity of emotion, whispered speech, or loss of all communicative function;
6. memory impairment or memory loss.

The *vertebro-basilar* system of arteries supplies blood primarily to the posterior regions of the brain. Occlusion here may produce a highly variable set of symptoms (see chapter 3). For now, be aware that a stroke in this system may—

1. produce a variety of visual disturbances, including impairment of coordination of the eyes;
2. impair sensation of heat and cold;

3. impair the ability to read and or name objects;
4. produce vertigo;
5. disturb balance;
6. create paralysis of the limbs, face, or tongue.

The signs and symptoms of a stroke in this arterial distribution are so highly variable, and often subtle, that small strokes are sometimes missed by trained medical practitioners. It may seem that an individual is displaying symptoms of confusion or an emotional disorder. Or it may appear that their balance is impaired due to disease of the inner ear. Unfortunately, these cerebrovascular accidents, if subtle, may go unrecognized for several years. The affected person may lose valuable time when rehabilitative efforts might have proven beneficial.

# Cerebral Hemorrhages

Approximately 10 percent of all strokes that occur in the United States each year are the result of a cerebral hemorrhage. Unlike other types of cerebrovascular accidents, the frequency of these episodes has not declined over the last 20 years.

Cerebral hemorrhage is the one type of stroke that occurs in young persons, as well as in individuals 50 and over. Younger victims usually suffer hemorrhage as a result of an anatomic abnormality of a cerebral vessel. They may be born with this problem or develop it early in life and the malformation may rupture at any time. There appears to be a tendency for the hemorrhage to occur during times of stress and strain, probably as the result of a sudden rise in arterial blood pressure.

Older persons who experience cerebral hemorrhage commonly suffer from hypertension, atherosclerosis, and the degenerative vacular changes that predispose to the formation of thrombi and emboli. It is unclear why some people suffer a rupture of a cerebral vessel while others develop clots. Unfortunately, in both younger and older persons, cerebral hemorrhage is often far more serious than either thrombosis or embolism.

Cerebral injury due to intracerebral bleeding results from the damaging effect of blood on the brain's neurological cells.

The brain is exquisitely sensitive to the presence of blood in the tissues—a decidedly abnormal occurrence. Blood produces a mass effect that puts abnormal pressure on the neurons and distorts their normal architecture. It also prevents oxygen and nutrients from passing from the bloodstream to the cells.

Bleeding into the brain looks like bleeding into other tissues of the body. After a period of minutes the blood will form a hard clot and active bleeding will stop. Over a period of months the dark clot slowly recedes, breaks down, and is absorbed by the body's white blood cells *(macrophages)*. In about a year the site of injury will resemble a small, slit-shaped cavity with orange borders.

Like thrombosis and embolism, the severity of a stroke caused by cerebral hemorrhages is determined by the size of the injury and the area of the brain that is affected. Small hemorrhages in the surface areas of the cerebrum may produce mild impairment. Large areas of bleeding, or injury to the body's vital centers for breathing and cardiac function are often fatal.

The death rate due to cerebral hemorrhages is quite high; there's a forty percent fatality rate within the first month. In general, the longer the period of coma or altered consciousness, the more grave the prognosis. Nevertheless, survival and recovery is possible. Agnes DeMille's book *Reprieve—A Memoire,* is the story of a cerebral hemorrhage and subsequent recovery.

The signs and symptoms of cerebral hemorrhages vary according to the size and site of injury, so that extremely small hemorrhages may go undetected. In the *putamen,* an area relatively deep within the brain substance where the majority of hemorrhages apparently occur, it is common for symptoms to develop while the individual is awake and active. At first there may be a pervasive feeling that something is definitely wrong. Weakness may develop and increase progressively. Loss of vision, sensation, poor balance, and difficulty communicating may develop fairly rapidly. Often the symptoms worsen until the individual lapses into a coma.

Hemorrhages in other areas of the brain may produce a sudden, overwhelming headache. Pain may be felt around one eye and there will likely be a loss of vision. When the hemorrhage affects the *cerebellum*, which lies in the back of the skull, it is common for there to be severe dizziness with nausea, difficulty standing, poor balance, and vomiting.

Symptoms such as a transitory loss of consciousness, disorientation, convulsions, headaches, and coma, are examples of alterations in normal consciousness, and require prompt medical attention. Persons with high blood pressure should be particularly alert to these signs.

The treatment for cerebral hemorrhages involves medical and sometimes surgical intervention. Due to the advent of *computerized axial tomography*, often abbreviated as the *CAT scan*, or *CT scan*, more efficient and accurate diagnoses of these strokes is possible. After the diagnosis is made, absolute bed rest is essential. The individual should also remain in a quiet environment, have limited visitors, and be monitored regularly by the medical staff. There is always the danger of suffering a repeat episode of bleeding, potentially fatal abnormal heart rhythms, and other complications. Blood pressure should be controlled cautiously, modest fluid intake must be carefully maintained, and measures must be taken to reduce elevated intracerebral pressure.

Other preventive and supportive measures may be required. Antacids and cimetidine (a drug which inhibits stomach acid production) are commonly employed to prevent gastrointestinal ulcers—a possible complication of cerebrovascular accidents. A high fiber diet with a stool softener may be helpful to prevent constipation. Straining to produce bowel movements can increase cerebral pressure or produce dangerous abnormal cardiac rhythms. Anticonvulsant medications and sedatives may also be needed.

There are experimental drugs such as tranexamic acid and aminocaproic acid that may be helpful in preventing the cerebral clot from dislodging. Special elastic stockings may be worn to prevent the formation of new clots in the legs. These have the potential of traveling to the lungs to impair respiration.

In some cases surgery to prevent additional bleeding and to evacuate clotted blood may be indicated. Studies evaluating the effectiveness of surgery for cerebral hemorrhages have produced somewhat conflicting results. So far there is no fixed rule indicating who should have cerebral surgery. The decision in each case will depend on the particular medical problems involved and the expertise and orientation of the medical practitioners.

Remember, a cerebral hemorrhage is an emergency. If you suspect that your symptoms may be due to this potentially life-threatening problem, get immediate medical attention. Chapters 3 and 5 cover in more detail the warning signs of a stroke and emergency procedures.

# To Review

1. The deficits produced by a cerebrovascular accident are due to injury to the highly specialized regions of the human brain that control different body parts and functions.

2. The largest and most developmentally advanced portion of the brain is the cerebrum, the site of the majority of strokes. The cerebrum is divided into two identical hemispheres; the majority of cerebral strokes occur in one or the other hemisphere, but not both.

3. Deficits from cerebral injury include partial or complete paralysis; impairment of vision, touch, and other sensation; loss of communicative function; and alteration of normal mentation. Individuals with right-sided cerebral injury may be impulsive and unaware of the left side of their body; persons with left-sided cerebral injury may have deficits in language function and display a slow and hesitant personality.

4. Strokes affecting the deep brain centers that control the heart, lungs, and other vital systems usually produce death. Strokes that involve the surface areas of the brain (cerebral cortex) produce specific deficits based on the location and extent of injury.

5. Lacunar strokes commonly affect motor function. They may be subtle and usually do not affect mental functioning.

6. The majority of strokes occur in the distribution of the middle cerebral artery and its branches. Other vessels, however, may become occluded and produce a cerebrovascular accident. The signs and symptoms of a stroke due to occlusion of vessels other than the MCA may be highly varied. The principal ones have been listed in this chapter.

7. About ten percent of strokes are caused by the rupture of a blood vessel in the brain and are called cerebral

hemorrhages. Atherosclerosis and high blood pressure are important underlying factors in this type of stroke. Young persons who suffer cerebral hemorrhages often have anatomic abnormalities of the blood vessel(s) that supply the brain.

8. Symptoms of a cerebral hemorrhage include excruciating headaches, a sudden loss of consciousness, and an abrupt onset of one of the other signs of strokes already mentioned. This is an emergency that requires immediate medical care (see chapter 5).

# 3

# Warning Signs

The warning signs of a stroke are the result of a partial or transient reduction of blood flow to the brain. The specific symptoms that are experienced relate to the highly specialized architecture of the central nervous system (see chapter 2). Understanding and recognizing these warning signs is important because many cerebrovascular accidents can be prevented. If potentially significant symptoms are recognized, prompt medical and surgical intervention may be employed to reduce the risk of suffering a future stroke. Appropriate prior treatment may also be beneficial for reducing the severity of a stroke that does occur. There are preventive treatments and certain general life-style changes which, if instituted early in life, may reduce the overall risk of having a cerebrovascular accident (see chapter 4).

The signs and symptoms discussed in this chapter may also be observed in illnesses other than strokes: these include infections of many types and inflammation of the inner ear, *dementia* (senility), tumors, and seizures. Many of these problems can also be successfully treated, especially when therapy is instituted early in the disease process. Thus, early detection is important whether the following symptoms are warning signs of a stroke, or due to another medical disorder. If you note any of these signs or symptoms in yourself, or in someone you care about, get prompt medical attention.

28

# Transient Ischemic Attacks (TIAs)

The general consensus is that about half of all people who eventually suffer a stroke due to thrombosis and a smaller, but yet significant number who suffer a CVA due to embolism, have warning episodes called *transient ischemic attacks* (TIAs). These events are associated with an increased risk of sustaining a later, serious cerebrovascular accident. It is thought that within 5 years of having a TIA, $\frac{1}{3}$ to $\frac{1}{2}$ its victims will suffer a stroke.

Even more dramatic, possibly, is the fact that about $\frac{1}{2}$ of these cerebrovascular accidents occur within a year of the first TIA and about $\frac{1}{5}$ in the first month. It is, therefore, particularly important to seek medical treatment *promptly*, after noticing one or more of these symptoms. A significant number of individuals are at risk for having a stroke shortly after their first warning sign.

This is the story of an individual who noticed the warning signs typical of a transient ischemic attack. Unfortunately, like many, he spent some time ignoring these symptoms, risking a possibly serious cerebrovascular accident. However, he was lucky in the long run; he was able to get appropriate treatment and has not gone on to suffer a stroke.

I first noticed that something wasn't right in May, when I had a few strange episodes. The first of which consisted of getting light-headed and losing the sight temporarily in my left eye. I also had some difficulty with my balance and felt like I needed to hold on to the living room easy chair to stand up. When I tried to walk I needed to lean my hands against the wall. The entire event lasted only five to ten minutes. I felt fine afterward and forgot about it.

About a week later it happened again. This time I was with my wife and we were shopping in the supermarket. She saw me losing my balance and said, "John look out, you're going to fall." I heard her, but had some difficulty answering. I must have stared at her with a blank look on my face for a few moments. She tried to shake me and at the same time hold me up. I was trying to keep my balance and collect my thoughts. I knew that I wanted to say something, but I couldn't get the words out. In a few minutes, though, my mind cleared up and things seemed normal. This time the whole thing probably lasted only two or three minutes.

She wanted me to go right to the doctor, but I didn't want to go. I thought that it might have been due to something I'd eaten for breakfast. You know, low blood sugar, or something like that.

A few weeks went by and I felt just fine. But, then it happened again. This time I was at work. I had been concentrating on an important report about a new sales program and again lost sight in one eye. My right arm and hand seemed to have pins and needles and I couldn't hold on to the pen. Again, I was better within a short time, but this time I was frightened. I thought that I might have brain cancer or epilepsy. After grappling with the prospect that I might be seriously ill, I made an appointment to see my doctor.

He thought that it was sufficiently serious that he wanted me to come in right away. He gave me a thorough examination, some blood tests, an *electrocardiogram*, and X rays, and told me that I should see a neurologist. In the meantime, I started taking medication that he prescribed. From what I understand, I had experienced the warning signs of a stroke. I had not actually sustained a true stroke, because there was no permanent injury that we could identify. But, I know now that they were signals that a stroke might be on the way and I'm glad that I went for treatment.

Transient ischemic attacks are different from strokes in that they do not produce demonstrable signs and symptoms of permanent brain injury. They are episodes of disruption of normal brain functioning that come on quickly and resolve spontaneously. TIA episodes may last from a few seconds to

24 hours although most last only 5 to 10 minutes. Generally, symptoms that last more than 24 hours are considered indicative of a minor stroke.

In the general public about 1 person in 1,000 is thought to have a TIA. But, in a group over the age of 65, this frequency goes up, so that as many as 100 in 1,000 will be expected to experience these symptoms. This is not surprising, since the frequency of strokes also goes up with advancing years and we know that TIAs and CVAs are associated. People who have TIAs have a generally shorter life expectancy and a greater risk of having a stroke than the average person and should, therefore, seek medical attention.

Like a stroke, the symptoms of a TIA depend on the specific geographic region of the brain that is affected. In general, these symptoms refer to—

1. diminished blood supply to the territory supplied by the middle cerebral artery or one of its branches. The reduction in blood flow may be due to partial occlusion of the artery itself, or due to disease within the carotid arteries of the neck (see chapter 2).

2. impaired blood flow to the vertebral and/or *basilar arteries* that supply blood to the posterior (rear) areas of the brain (see chapter 2 for a discussion of the functions of this portion of the brain).

# Carotid Artery Disease

The example that we have just presented involves symptoms that are typical of partial occlusion of the left carotid artery. Remember that blood from the heart enters the *middle cerebral artery (MCA)* by passing through the carotid system. Thus, partial occlusion of the carotid artery will temporarily produce symptoms that are also characteristic of reduced blood flow in the area of the MCA. This is probably the most common type of TIA, producing symptoms such as—

1. loss of vision in one eye (on the same side as the artery that is narrowed);

2. blindness over half of the field of vision, usually involving the affected side of the neck;
3. difficulty focusing or concentrating on objects in the visual field;
4. impaired sensation, such as numbness, tingling, or complete anesthesia of the face, arm, or leg on the *opposite* of the involved blood vessel;
5. weakness or paralysis of the muscles of the face, arm, or leg on the *opposite* side of the narrowed artery;
6. difficulty with language and communication, such as stammering, becoming unable to use appropriate words, having difficulty uttering any words, using a confused sentence structure, becoming unable to understand speech or being unable to write and do arithmetic calculations;
7. impaired recognition of familiar objects or individuals, although voice recognition may be intact;
8. inability to perform commonplace activities, such as dressing, grooming, or relatively simple tasks of daily living.

The example we have presented is typical of a TIA that results from progressive thrombosis of the carotid artery on the left side of the neck. An embolus affecting the same distribution would also produce similar symptoms. As circulation is reduced, blood does not reach the left middle cerebral artery in sufficient quantity to maintain normal neurological functioning. Disorders of language are typical of TIAs affecting the *left* cerebral hemisphere, since about half of all left-handed individuals have their primary language centers located in the left side of the brain.

In this case history, the difficulty walking and standing was likely due to weakness of the right leg. The dizziness and light-headedness that often accompanies any TIA was also probably a contributing factor. The numbness and tingling of the right arm, however, is typical of an impaired blood supply to the left cerebral hemisphere and a strong indicator that the *left* carotid artery or MCA may be diseased.

After hearing about the recurrent episodes of weakness and difficulty with speech and language, it was appropriate for the physician to encourage a prompt evaluation of the problem. The fact that the symptoms resolved completely is not indicative of a benign condition. It is impossible to predict whether the next episode would have been a devastating cerebrovascular accident, or whether it might occur in a relatively short period of time. Thus, prompt evaluation and treatment was essential.

The reason why some people have loss of vision in one eye during these episodes is not entirely understood. Some feel that it occurs when small clots break away from atheromas in the carotid artery and impair blood flow in the vessels that supply the *ophthalmic nerve*. Others feel that emboli produce blindness by affecting the retinal blood vessels directly, as they pass through the eye. And others hypothesize that both mechanisms may be at work simultaneously. For whatever reason, it is important to report any alteration of normal vision to your medical practitioner immediately.

Be aware that it is unusual for a TIA to produce more than a momentary loss of consciousness. Such attacks are more likely to be due to excessively high or low blood sugar, heart disease, epilepsy, and certain less common medical conditions. A sudden drop in blood pressure (particularly associated with a change of posture) or a fainting spell may also mimic the signs of a TIA. The underlying cause of these episodes is different from that of a transient ischemic attack.

# Vertral-Basilar Artery Disease

The two vertebral arteries run next to the spinal bones at each side of the neck. They feed into one vessel, the basilar artery, which supplies blood to the inferior (lower portion) and posterior (rear) areas of the brain. Transient ischemic attacks may result from a narrowing of either of the vertebral arteries or the basilar artery. Sometimes arthritis of the bones of the neck may pinch a vertebral artery already narrowed by atherosclerosis. This, in turn, blocks circulation, making a TIA more likely. Here, for example, is the story of one man who had such a problem.

My husband was a healthy man well into his seventies who came from a family where everyone seemed to live well into old age. He considered himself a vigorous person who enjoyed heavy work. He had labored his entire life in a factory and saw retirement as a way to have more time for hobbies and work around the house. But, he never really thought of slowing down.

After a year of healthy and relatively happy retirement, he seemed to be in better spirits than I had seen him in years. He enjoyed working around the house, puttering in the shop, and keeping the grounds tended.

In February he had a short, but very frightening episode of dizziness and felt like the world was spinning around. You know, like being on a ride in the amusement park where they spin you until you get very dizzy. But, this was happening while he was chopping wood, not because he was on a ride.

The feeling didn't last all that long and he thought that it might have been something he ate, a touch of the flu, or a problem with his eyes. A few days later it happened again, and this time he threw up. His vision was all blurred. He told me about it and we decided he should go to the doctor.

The doctor admitted him into the hospital and did some tests. At first he thought that it might be a problem in his ears. But the tests showed a pinched blood vessel in the neck, possibly due to his arthritis. The doctor explained that when my husband was chopping wood his neck would move back and forth probably hindering blood flow.

The doctor put him on some medicines and he has been fine since. I make sure that he takes his pills and try to keep him away from the wood pile. It's not easy to keep him from hard work. He says that he'll keep working hard around the house and keep on his medicines.

The symptoms just described are common to *vertebral artery insufficiency,* a condition that may produce TIAs. Some typical manifestations of this disorder are—

1. dizziness;
2. *vertigo* (the sensation that one's surroundings are spinning);
3. blurred vision, double vision, blind spots, or vision that seems to be suddenly dimmed;
4. partial or complete blindness in one or both eyes;
5. clumsy movements of the hands;
6. difficulty judging distances when trying to co-ordinate limb movements *(dysmetria);*
7. difficulty maintaining balance while standing or walking *(ataxia);*
8. incoordination of the muscles of the lips, mouth, tongue, and vocal cords producing slurred speech *(dysarthria);*
9. drooling saliva from the mouth and difficulty swallowing *(dysphagia);*
10. localized numbness, typically involving the mouth or lips; temporary shifting numbness over different areas of the body *(parasthesia);* or almost complete body numbness *(total body anesthesia);*
11. "drop attacks" where there is a sudden loss of muscular and postural control resulting in collapse (the individual is fully awake and conscious, but loses all postural control); or an incomplete version of the "drop attack" in which there is shifting partial paralysis or weakness of the arms or legs;
12. loss of memory *(amnesia)* that gradually improves.

# The Subclavian Steal Syndrome

This is an *uncommon* condition in which there is a narrowing of the subclavian artery that runs under the *clavicle* or collarbone. Symptoms result when the arm and shoulder on the side of the narrowed vessel are exercised. Typically movement of the arm produces numbness and weakness, and a light-headed sensation. Other signs already presented that are typical of TIAs may also be present.

In the *subclavian steal syndrome* blood is "stolen" from the brain and delivered to the exercised arm. It is a warning sign that advanced atherosclerosis may be present in arteries throughout the body. Since this includes cerebral vessels, measures should be taken to prevent a future stroke.

The "Taxi Man's Collar" syndrome is a variant of both the subclavian steal syndrome and basilar-vertebral artery insufficiency. This occurs when the neck is turned quickly producing momentary compression of the carotid artery. In turn this causes an interference with the normal blood pressure control center in the neck, a rapid drop in blood pressure, and a loss of consciousness. The name originated when taxi cab drivers reported an alteration of consciousness when turning their head to see passengers in the backseat.

# Small Strokes

In certain instances, the symptoms of a transient ischemic attack may not resolve in twenty-four hours. Instead, they may last a day or more, completely resolving or leaving only minor deficits. In some cases, the impairment is barely noticeable. These minor episodes are important warning signs that a more serious cerebrovascular accident may soon occur.

This is the story of a small stroke that went untreated. As a result, a full-blown cerebrovascular accident occurred.

In 1946, I was twenty-three and just out of the army. I had returned from Germany and was helping my family work the family farm we had in Ohio. My grandmother and grandfather lived with us and also enjoyed working the long days characteristic of farm life.

I had always remembered my grandfather as a hardworking, bear of a man. I don't think that he ever really took a vacation in his entire life. Farmers just don't do that, you know. But, when I returned from Europe, it seemed as though my grandfather had changed. No one else in the family seemed to notice it, but I did.

Then, one morning he awoke with a slight droop on the right side of his face and some weakness in his right arm. My grandmother told him that he had a stroke during the night, but my grandfather wouldn't listen to her. He just went off to the barn to do his usual chores. I think that he was frightened and didn't want to admit that something serious was happening.

My mother and father were nervous about it and told him to go see the doctor. He wouldn't do that, but agreed to spend a few days in bed—resting up—as he called it. He slept a lot, but never seemed to regain his old self. His right arm remained weak and somewhat clumsy and the droop never fully left his face.

I moved away a few months later. It was time, I felt, for me to seek fame and fortune in California. One day I received word that Grandpa had had a major stroke and was paralyzed. Looking back, it was clear that he had had a little stroke during the summer.

A month after his big stroke he was dead. The doctor said that he had suffered another stroke, or maybe a heart attack. He said that heart attacks often happen to people who have strokes. He also said that my grandfather probably didn't have any pain when he died, but I remember crying when I heard the news. I wished there was something we could have done after that first small stroke.

A small stroke that resolves completely is called *RIND (Reversible Ischemic Neurological Deficit)*. If the episode lasts more than seventy-two hours and produces some minor neurological dysfunction, it is called *PRIND (Partially Reversible Ischemic Neurological Deficit)*. The case just described would probably fall into this latter category, since the right arm remained weak and there was partial paralysis of the face. In both a RIND or PRIND the mechanism of injury is the same as that for a full stroke or TIA: blood flow to the tissues of the brain is reduced below the critical level necessary for normal neurological functioning.

The exact frequency of small strokes is not known. In all probability many individuals who are in the ninth or tenth decade of life, particularly if they live alone, may have these episodes and not report them to a medical practitioner. Left untreated, however, a small stroke may be the harbinger of a large and potentially devastating cerebrovascular accident.

There seems to be little argument over the notion that the risk of having a serious stroke increases after one or more small episodes. Estimates for this vary, but according to a 1981 report of the National Survey on Strokes, it may be as much as *tenfold*. If many individuals are unaware of their small stroke, or if they do not report it to a medical practitioner, the actual figure may be higher.

Fortunately, there are a number of medical and surgical treatments available that attempt to prevent small strokes from becoming large ones. There are also changes that can be made in diets and in the patterns of daily living, which may also be helpful. Remember, slight changes in behavior and personality, weakness or sensory changes in the extremities, lapses in memory, impairment of speech and language, or abnormalities of spatial perception and vision are potential signs of a small stroke. They should be reported to a medical practitioner promptly and given a thorough evaluation. There are strategies currently available for preventing TIAs and small strokes from becoming serious and debilitating ones (see chapter 4).

# Important Medical Terms

The signs and symptoms of a stroke or transient ischemic attack have medical terms that may be new to individuals who have no medical training. Since they may be employed by medical practitioners, it is worthwhile to attain an understanding of the terminology. The following is a summary of some of the more commonly used vocabulary:

1. *Amnesia*. Memory loss
2. *Anosognosia*. Denial of illness

3. *Apraxia*. Inability to use common objects in the absence of significant muscular weakness or incoordination
4. *Asomatognosia*. Unawareness of part of the body
5. *Ataxia*. Muscular incoordination, particularly when standing or walking
6. *Claudication*. Cramping pain with exercise
7. *Dysarthria*. Poor coordination of the physical structures of the mouth and neck that produce speech
8. *Dysmetria*. Improper measurement of distance and spatial relationships
9. *Dysphagia*. Difficulty swallowing
10. *Hemianesthesia*. Loss of sensation over half (either the right or left side) of the body, including touch, temperature, and pain awareness
11. *Hemianopia*. Loss of perception of one side of the visual field
12. *Hemiparesis*. Weakness over half of the body (either the right or left side)
13. *Hemiplegia*. Paralysis over half of the body (either the right or left side)
14. *Monocular Blindness*. Loss of vision in one eye
15. *Parasthesia*. Numbness or tingling ("pins and needles")
16. *Scotoma*. Blind spot

# To Review

1. Warning signs of a potential future stroke occur in a significant percentage of individuals who later go on to suffer a full cerebrovascular accident.

2. Stroke warning signs are commonly the result of arterial disease that intermittently and for a relatively short period of time reduces blood flow to areas of the brain.

3. Transient ischemic attacks (TIAs) are short episodes of neurological malfunctioning, which produce symptoms such as weakness, loss of normal sensation, difficulty speaking or understanding others, loss of vision, or poor balance

and coordination. While these episodes do not produce permanent injury or disability, they are the harbingers of possible future strokes and require medical attention.

4. It is essential to get *prompt* medical attention after experiencing a transient ischemic attack, since some individuals will suffer a stroke within thirty days.

5. TIAs and small strokes may also occur because of disease in noncerebral blood vessels; that is, carotid and vertebral arteries of the neck or the subclavian artery within the chest.

6. Know the warning signs of cerebrovascular accidents and be able to recognize them in yourself or in others. Note that these symptoms may appear in conditions other than a TIA or small stroke. In most cases, they, too, require prompt medical evaluation and possible treatment.

# 4

# Preventing Strokes

Forty years ago, when President Franklin Delano Roosevelt suffered a stroke, few physicians felt that there was much that could have been done to prevent his illness. At that point treatments for hypertension, atherosclerosis, and other underlying conditions that predispose to cerebrovascular accidents were virtually nonexistent.

Today, this has changed. There are a variety of medical and surgical interventions that can reduce the risk of sustaining a serious stroke. There are treatments that can also reduce the severity of CVAs that do occur. While these approaches are relatively new, it is hoped that their implementation in the general population will produce a reduction in the frequency of serious stroke episodes. In fact, this may already be occurring. Recent statistics indicate that the overall incidence of strokes has declined in the last decade, possibly as a result of the improved treatment of conditions like hypertension, coronary artery disease, and diabetes. Individual modifications of life-style may have also been relevant to the reduction in stroke frequency. It is hoped that continued changes in life-styles coupled with early recognition and preventive therapy will further reduce the future incidence of cerebrovascular accidents.

## Treatment of Transient Ischemic Attacks

Most medical professionals consider transient ischemic attacks to be a warning sign of an impending stroke (see chapter 3). And, after a TIA the majority of these professionals advise some form of preventive therapy. There is, however, some disagreement as to the exact type of treatment that is best. Discuss with your medical provider the issue and choose the approach that best fits your needs.

Three principal avenues of preventive therapy have been developed. The first is the use of aspirin and other *platelet-inhibiting drugs* to prevent the formation of potentially dangerous blood clots. As was previously mentioned, the creation of clots is an important event in both thrombus and embolus formation. These drugs prevent blood from coagulating by reducing the adhesiveness of small cells in the bloodstream *(platelets)*, which stick together to initiate blood clotting. Platelets have a particular tendency to stick to damaged areas within the vessels where atheromas have formed. In this situation, they are not protecting the body from hemorrhages, but clump together inappropriately to clog arteries. They may also form in an area of atheroma and break off, traveling downstream to obstruct another blood vessel.

A second preventive strategy is to use *anticoagulant drugs*, which inhibit clotting by a different mechanism. These medicines interfere with the activity of clotting factors—chemicals in the liquid portion of the blood that are essential for the coagulation procedure. These drugs lengthen the time required for a clot to form. In general, anticoagulants have a potent effect on the clotting process and may be more dangerous than platelet inhibitors when used on a long-term basis. There is the risk that when taking medications abnormal bleeding may occur spontaneously or in the face of minor trauma.

A third method is to employ *surgery* to remove clots from narrowed arteries and to repair damaged blood vessels where clots may be predisposed to form. The most common type of surgery for this purpose is performed on narrowed areas in the carotid arteries of the neck *(carotid endarterectomy);* this is now the second most commonly performed vascular surgery in the United States.

During carotid surgery the diseased vessel is opened, the clot removed, and an artificial graft put in its place. Continued advances in performing the operation have been made over the last 20 years to improve the safety of the procedure.

At the Mayo Clinic in Rochester, Minnesota, for instance, surgeons claim an operative mortality rate of 1.5 percent and a 1-percent risk of inducing a stroke.

*Superficial temporal artery bypass* is a new alternative surgical therapy for preventing future strokes. The idea behind the procedure is to take blood from superficial vessels in the scalp and reroute it into cerebral vessels. An opening in the skull must be made for this purpose.

Research is underway to determine which individuals are most likely to benefit from these surgical approaches. As with coronary bypass surgery and other new procedures, there is always a period of time in which it is necessary to study an intervention and assess its appropriate use.

There is also disagreement among medical scientists as to the most appropriate type of medical therapy for inhibiting blood clotting. Studies comparing the effectiveness of daily doses of aspirin, aspirin with other drugs such as sulphinpyrazone (Anturane $^T$) and Dipyridamole (Persantine), or sulphinpyrazone and Dipyridamole alone, have been carried out. Aspirin, as already mentioned, inhibits blood clotting by affecting platelets. Sulphinpyrazone and dipyridamole interfere with blood clotting by a different mechanism, not yet completely understood.

The results of the use of these different drugs for the prevention of strokes have been mixed, but tend to favor the use of aspirin as a single medication. To date, the greatest benefit from this approach has been noted in men. Aspirin is relatively safe, inexpensive, and appears to be as effective as using a multiple drug regimen.

Further study is needed to compare the effectiveness of surgery as opposed to drug therapy. While the risk and cost of surgery may be greater, it offers the potential of effecting a cure. In other words, after surgery there may be no need for taking daily doses of medication—an activity that itself involves both risk and cost.

Although there is uncertainty at this time whether medical therapy or surgery is best for preventing recurrent transient ischemic attacks (and possible future strokes), physicians generally feel that *some therapy is indicated*. Left untreated, a significant number of individuals who suffer from TIAs will go on to have disabling, possibly fatal, cerebrovascular accidents.

# Treating Hypertension

Virtually all medical scientists agree that hypertension (high blood pressure) is the single most important risk factor predisposing to cerebrovascular accidents. Hypertension produces direct injury to blood vessels, increasing the likelihood of cerebral hemorrhages. In addition, evidence implicates its role in aggravating the atherosclerotic process (hardening of the arteries) by driving fatty substances into the arterial walls, making them brittle, narrow, and rigid.

At least one third to half of all individuals who have a stroke suffer from hypertension. In people with severe hypertensive disease, the risk of having a CVA is increased at least sixfold. It is also a significant risk factor for both women and men.

High blood pressure that continues over a number of years also damages the heart. If a stroke occurs, the already compromised heart will be less capable of delivering needed blood to the tissues of the brain. This may further aggravate the severity of the episode.

Treating hypertension with appropriate medication may reduce the risk of a stroke, particularly in younger persons. This had been confirmed in studies with individuals who have mild, moderate, or markedly high blood pressure. Successful treatment has been shown to reduce the risk of all types of strokes—cerebral hemorrhage, thrombosis, and embolism. While there is debate as to the most appropriate level of blood pressure for a given individual, there seems to be little doubt that persistent high blood pressure should be lowered. Moreover, there is little argument that hypertension is a risk factor in other disorders: cardiac and kidney disease and eye illnesses, for instance.

Franklin Roosevelt suffered from persistently elevated blood pressure that very likely was the underlying cause of his fatal cerebral hemorrhage. Unfortunately, effective drug treatment for his disease was not available in his day. Now, however, this has changed. There are many different types of medications that effectively control blood pressure so that there is no excuse for continuing to live with hypertension.

If you do not know whether you have high blood

pressure, get it checked. This can be done by your family medical provider, local clinic or hospital, or through a variety of community groups.

Some people mistakenly stop taking their blood pressure medications because they encounter an unpleasant side effect or because they feel that they are in good health and do not need their treatment. It is important to remember that hypertension is usually a *silent disease* so that there are usually no discernible symptoms until *permanent* damage has been done to the body's vital organs. For most individuals medical therapy is needed for the rest of one's life.

If you have stopped taking your medicines because of an unpleasant side effect, return to your medical practitioner for care. There are many different medications available and your treatment can be tailored to your individual needs. It is now possible for individuals to remain on antihypertensive therapy for a lifetime with a minimum of unpleasant side effects.

Combining a variety of interventions like relaxation; meditation; biofeedback; stress reduction; dietary control, particularly the restriction of excessive salt intake; regular exercise; and appropriate medication, are now considered the optimal forms of blood pressure control. Caffeine found in coffee, nonherbal teas, and some carbonated beverages raises blood pressure so that limiting the intake of these substances can also make a difference. In some cases, life-style changes can reduce or eliminate the need for taking daily medication. No matter how one views it, high blood pressure should be controlled. It may be the single most important factor for reducing the risk of having a cerebrovascular accident.

# Diabetes Mellitus

A number of studies have implicated *diabetes mellitus* as a risk factor for stroke. In Israel, for instance, one study noted that twenty percent of those who suffered a cerebrovascular accident were diabetic. It appears that diabetes may produce as much as fourfold increase in the risk of having a CVA.

One mechanism by which diabetes predisposes to strokes may be by rapidly accelerating atherosclerosis. As fats collect in the diabetic's bloodstream, they become deposited on the arterial walls, and increase the likelihood of both thrombus and embolus formation.

Additional study is needed to assess the role of blood sugar control as a method for preventing cerebrovascular accidents. At this point most experts in the field feel that maintenance of blood sugar within the normal range is a worthwhile goal. Normal levels can be obtained through a varied program of exercise, stress reduction, dietary modification, and medication.

Getting checked for diabetes is simple, inexpensive, and should be part of the regular physical examination performed by your health care provider. The diagnosis and appropriate treatment of diabetes mellitus at different ages of life is undergoing some debate in medical circles. For older persons, with diabetes that *starts in adulthood*, a program of dietary control, exercise, and appropriate life-style changes may be all that is needed. Other individuals may require the addition of oral medication. Insulin injection is now not currently thought to be needed for the majority of adult onset diabetics.

As in our previous discussion of hypertension, it appears that the appropriate control of blood sugar is an important part of a stroke prevention program. If it appears that you have diabetes, measures to treat your condition—based on your age, life-style, and individual physiology—should be taken. The patterns of living that help to maintain normal blood pressure and blood sugar produce positive health practices in general. Discuss the appropriate measures with your family medical practitioner.

# Hyperlipidemia, Obesity, and Heart Disease

It has been known for some time that elevated blood levels of fats and cholesterol (together called *lipids*) produce an increased risk of heart disease by accelerating the atherosclerotic process. It seems that a similar response to *hyperlipidemia* occurs in the brain, increasing the risk of producing strokes. In other words, evidence suggests that a similar process produces both heart disease and strokes; and that similar strategies for prevention will be beneficial.

Researchers in the internationally recognized study at

Framingham in Massachusetts have carefully studied a large number of individuals as they have aged. This study identified a link between elevated levels of blood *(serum)* cholesterol and strokes in men between the ages of 50 and 59 years of age. No similar correlation was noted for women, or for older participants. However, many scientists feel that elevation of serum lipids above normal may be a significant risk factor for cerebrovascular accidents, particularly when combined with other risk factors like hypertension and diabetes.

Many types of heart disease appear to increase the risk for strokes. These include diseases like coronary insufficiency, angina, and myocardial infarction (heart attack), which are related to atherosclerosis. These conditions may increase the likelihood of suffering a stroke from 2½ to tenfold. Rheumatic heart disease and *atrial fibrillation*—cardiac conditions not directly related to atherosclerosis—may also increase the risk of strokes up to twenty-fivefold.

Also linked is the question of obesity. Being overweight is known to be a risk factor in hypertension and diabetes and many obese persons have hyperlipidemia. As yet it is not possible to say whether obesity is itself a risk factor for strokes, but it is so often associated with other risk factors that getting down to normal weight should be part of a complete stroke prevention program.

Interestingly, the subject of correct weight at various ages is currently under intensive scrutiny. Some medical scientists favor moving up the acceptable weight, particularly after age seventy-five, and revising the weight tables, in general.

While further study may be needed to develop accurate weight tables, most physicians encourage the loss of excess pounds. In almost all areas of health, and in the daily enjoyment of living, obesity is a physical, emotional, and social burden. Losing excess weight is often a way to control diabetes, high blood pressure, and hyperlipidemia. It is also known to be a significant risk factor for heart attacks, accidents, arthritis, possibly cancer, and many other common illnesses that plague mankind. If you are overweight, we suggest that you get into a program to lose and keep off excess pounds. Not only may this be beneficial for reducing your risk of suffering a CVA, but it can improve your total outlook on life.

Older persons, who may be at the greatest risk for strokes, should obtain regular medical checkups that include an examination of the heart. In general, this can be performed safely and relatively inexpensively in a physician's office with a thorough physical examination, appropriate blood tests, and an electrocardiogram. Two specific types of heart disease are known to greatly increase the risk of producing a cerebrovascular accident: atheriosclerotic heart disease and *valvular heart disease*. Both conditions can be treated with existing medical technology, and you should be checked for the possible presence of these conditions.

# Oral Contraceptives (Birth Control Pills)

Taking oral contraceptives, particularly those with a high estrogen content (which were more commonly prescribed when oral contraceptives were first put on the market), has been shown to increase the risk of having a future stroke.

The risk of having a stroke while taking oral contraceptives increases as women of childbearing age become older. Thus, the risk for a woman in her twenties is considerably lower than for a woman in her forties. Estrogen replacement, when taken for postmenopausal symptoms, and to prevent *osteoporosis* (decrease in bone mass producing fragility, generally resulting from age-related disturbances in bone metabolism), has not been shown to increase the risk of cerebrovascular accidents.

Smoking while taking the pill appears to further increase the risk of having a stroke. According to the surgeon general, a woman who takes the pill *and* smokes may have a two-hundredfold increase in the risk of suffering a CVA.

# Smoking

The statistical significance of data on smoking and cerebrovascular accidents is somewhat unclear. According to the Framingham study, men aged 50–59 who smoked more than 1 pack per day had a 2.2 times greater risk of having a CVA than nonsmokers of the same age.

Smoking is definitely known to increase the risk for heart attacks and probably plays a role in accelerating atherosclerosis. It may also produce diseases of the cerebral vasculature. It therefore seems prudent to reduce or eliminate smoking as a stroke prevention strategy. Contrary to some popular views, pipe and cigar smoking, as well as cigarettes, are known to be risk factors for heart and vascular disease. Chewing tobacco increases the risk of acquiring cancer of the mouth and neck. Evidence also mounts to implicate tobacco consumption in lung cancer; chronic obstructive pulmonary disease *(emphysema)*, diseases of the peripheral blood vessels, and so many other conditions that control of this common habit appears to be a worthwhile general health practice. It may also help to reduce the risk of having a cerebrovascular accident.

## Polycythemia

Increased blood viscosity *(polycythemia)*, has been shown to be a risk factor for coronary infarction (heart attacks) and, to a lesser extent, strokes. Under these circumstances blood flows sluggishly, increasing the likelihood of both thrombosis and embolism. It is also associated with certain chronic blood disorders and emphysema.

In the Framingham study, both men and women with relative polycythemia showed an increased risk for cerebrovascular accidents. At least one other study, which attempted to control the risk factors related to strokes, took measures to reduce abnormally high blood viscosity. Although additional work is needed, the results of that study indicate that there may be some benefit from treating polycythemia.

There are a number of ways to reduce the viscosity of blood. The simplest is a regular program of blood withdrawal *(phlebotomy)*. This is simple, safe, and virtually painless. Testing for polycythemia can be performed in a doctor's office with a blood test. If there appears to be an abnormality, discuss its potential significance and appropriate treatment with your medical provider.

## A Stroke Prevention Program

Clearly, the best strategy is to prevent strokes before they produce seriously disabling or fatal illnesses. Fortunately, the preventive measures discussed in this chapter are by and large safe and relatively inexpensive. The bulk of them will also improve overall health, outlook on life, and reduce the risk of suffering other generally common illnesses.

The following is a story of a stroke prevention program told by a family physician. It demonstrates that a reasonable program can be instituted that will not only reduce the risk for strokes, but produce other positive health results, as well.

John M. came to see me because he had been having intermittent episodes of weakness in his arm and loss of vision. I was immediately concerned that he might be having warning signs of blockage of an artery leading to the brain. I did a thorough physical examination, some laboratory tests, and special X rays and found that his right carotid artery was partially blocked. It was fairly clear that he had been having symptoms of a transient ischemic attack.

A number of options were open and we discussed them. The goal was to prevent a stroke that might come in the future. He could start taking daily doses of aspirin and other drugs to inhibit blood clotting, he could have surgery to repair the area of narrowing in his neck, and he could make some worthwhile changes in his life-style.

To start with, Mr. M. was overweight, a smoker, had high blood pressure, and the blood tests showed that he had abnormally high levels of cholesterol and fat circulating in his bloodstream. He had not participated in any regular exercise for many years.

We talked about the many possible risk factors that might be contributing to a possible future stroke. Certainly the fact that he had had a number of TIAs was an important warning sign to take seriously. We discussed the relevance of the partial blockage of the artery in his neck and of the other more general issues like smoking, obesity, and hyperlipidemia.

After talking about all of these things with Mr. M. and his wife, we decided to hold off on doing surgery for the partial blockage of his carotid artery.

The tests showed that about half of the normal blood flow was getting through and we probably had time to wait before doing an operation. But, I did feel that it was necessary to start doing something to prevent a CVA and he began taking aspirin on a daily basis. He also got involved in a program to stop smoking.

We also worked out a program of dietary modification. He and his wife agreed to eat fewer meals with red meat, butter, eggs, cheese, and other foods high in fat and cholesterol. They also began to add foods high in fiber, like bran cereal in the morning, whole wheat bread instead of white bread, and vegetables at two meals each day.

Since his blood pressure was 180/100 we began a program to lower it. This involved taking one daily dose of a *diuretic* (a medication that reduces blood pressure by increasing the urinary elimination of water and salt) and eliminating salty foods from his diet. He agreed that he would not add salt to his food at the table. The last element in our plan was to begin an exercise routine. We decided to start with a brisk and continuous walk for thirty minutes every day.

We are now about one year past his first TIA symptom and Mr. M. has not had a stroke. There is no way of knowing, for certain, whether he would have had a stroke without our program. But, the risk was there.

He also seems to feel better, generally. He has lost weight, quit his cigarette smoking, and improved his blood cholesterol and fat levels. These are worthwhile general health practices, anyway. He says that he has more energy and feels more fit generally, so our program has worked in a number of ways.

Mr. M.'s program involved minimal risk or financial cost. Other treatments, like surgical removal or repair of the diseased vessel in his neck and regular administration of anticoagulant medicines were not needed. While these interventions may be lifesaving for some individuals, they do involve certain risks and costs. The point is that a stroke prevention program should be tailored to the individual's needs and medical condition.

Scientific study is currently underway to evaluate the efficacy of stroke prevention. Many centers, in both North America and Europe, are attempting to look at this question in the hope of finding ways to reduce the frequency and risk of our number three killer.

For now, it seems prudent to avail oneself of the existing methods for treating hypertension, diabetes, and hyperlipidemia. The use of high dose estrogen oral contraceptives should be minimized particularly as women approach the upper limit of the childbearing years; smoking should be reduced or eliminated; and a regular program of physical exercise, stress reduction, and dietary control may also be helpful.

While Mr. M. waited until he had signs of a transient ischemic attack before seeing his medical practitioner, it is not necessary for others to do so. Life-style modifications should begin before troublesome symptoms are noted. Blood pressure, *serum glucose* (blood sugar), and serum lipids (fat and cholesterol in the blood) should be checked as part of a regular physical examination. An electrocardiogram, complete blood count, and certain other simple and relatively inexpensive tests can be performed by your family medical provider. The results of these tests plus a general assessment of your overall health status will allow you and your health practitioner to devise an appropriate stroke prevention program.

## To Review

1. A transient ischemic attack (see chapter 3) is an important warning sign of a possible future stroke; medical therapy or surgical intervention should be initiated, as deemed appropriate.

2. Hypertension is probably the single most important risk factor for strokes. Have your blood pressure checked; if it requires treatment, there are a variety of medications and life-style changes that can be effective for controlling it. Remember that hypertension is a silent disease. In most cases

symptoms do not appear until irreversible damage to the body's vital organs has already occurred.

3. Diabetes mellitus appears to be a risk factor for strokes. Blood sugar can be tested by your medical practitioner, and in many cases can be controlled by life-style changes. Insulin injections are not commonly needed for persons who become diabetic in adulthood.

4. Elevated blood levels of cholesterol and fat, obesity, and heart disease are known to increase the risk of cerebrovascular accidents. Evidence of these conditions can be noted on a regular physical examination by your medical practitioner, and should be treated with appropriate medical therapy and life-style changes.

5. Oral contraceptives, particularly when taken with high estrogen content by women in their late thirties and forties, increases the risk for strokes. Smoking while taking these pills further increases the risk.

5. Smoking is a risk factor in many serious illnesses and may be an important risk factor for strokes. If you smoke, consider beginning a program to reduce and hopefully eliminate your tobacco consumption habit. Pipe smoking, cigars, and chewing tobacco also contain definite health risks.

7. Polycythemia is a condition in which blood is abnormally viscous. A simple blood test can check for this condition. Appropriate therapy should be discussed with your health care provider.

8. A stroke prevention program is, in many respects, a positive overall health maintenance regimen. The life-style changes that can reduce the risk of sustaining a future stroke may also reduce the risk of suffering heart disease, cancer, and other common medical diseases. These general health practices may also be helpful for improving your overall well-being, energy, and enjoyment of life.

# 5

# The Stroke Emergency

A stroke is a sudden and often frightening medical situation and it is not surprising that many people are fearful that they will be unable to effectively cope with the emergency. They think they will panic or be otherwise unable to provide necessary medical support. However, with a little forethought and training, you can be prepared to take appropriate action.

For the most part, there is often nothing extremely complicated or magical about providing supportive aid. Common sense and a desire to help often leads one in the right direction. Calling for professional emergency assistance, holding the ill or injured person's hand and speaking in a quiet and calm tone are some simple actions that often are all that is needed.

As was pointed out (see chapter 2), the majority of strokes occur in the face of thrombosis or embolism of an artery. In these situations, appropriate emergency care involves getting the stroke victim safely and expeditiously to the emergency ward of a hospital. Only during severe cerebral hemorrhages will absolute speed and more aggressive medical intervention be needed. The techniques that may then be required, such as the treatment of shock and cardiopulmonary resuscitation are beyond the scope of this book. They should, in general, be learned through a course on emergency first aid and basic life support. Such training can be obtained through your local chapter of the American Red Cross and American Heart Association, hospital, and through a variety of community groups. We urge everyone to learn these potentially life-saving measures before an emergency arises. Fortunately, most strokes do not require this type of emergency care.

Be aware that in virtually all emergency situations, effective action requires keeping a clear and level head. Panic is an enemy that impairs appropriate first aid. Read the material in this chapter in order to understand how to deal with a stroke. Think through how you will get to the hospital, who you will call for help, and what you will do while help is on the way *before* a stroke emergency occurs.

## The Acute Stroke Episode

The signs and symptoms of an acute stroke (sometimes called a *stroke in evolution*), have already been described in the preceding chapters. They include an alteration of normal awake consciousness, difficulty communicating, partial or complete paralysis, disturbances of vision and sensation, and difficulty maintaining balance. In most cases, the symptoms are fairly obvious and the person who is affected knows that something extremely unusual and *wrong* is happening. Even though they may have difficulty speaking, they will probably know that they need emergency medical care and want you to get it for them.

During the period when the symptoms of a stroke are progressing (or "evolving"), your job is to provide general comfort, reassurance, and support. You should also make prompt and appropriate arrangements for transport to a nearby hospital emergency room. Third, you should provide basic measures to make the person comfortable while help is on the way. The following story, told by a woman whose husband suffered a stroke, is a good example of these three basic principles.

I was coming through the front door after work when I noticed that Bob had fallen to the floor. He was lying motionless next to the dining room table and didn't seem to respond when I called out to him. I was immediately alarmed, dropped my packages, and ran over to him. Nothing like this had ever happened to us before.

I gave him a little shake and looked into his eyes. He tried to speak to me, but only got out some unintelligible sounds. He was definitely awake though, which made me feel a lot better. I remember asking him, "Did you pass out?" He couldn't answer with words, but he made a kind of "no" motion with his left hand. Knowing that he hadn't passed out made me feel even more relieved.

I did notice that he was curled up on his right side. His arm was tucked under him and he was not moving. His face was drooping down on the right. Something told me that this wasn't a heart attack. He seemed to be breathing fairly normally and he had a pulse. He was pale, but he didn't seem to be in pain. I asked him if his chest hurt, and he made another "no" kind of motion with his left arm.

I didn't try to move him, but pulled the dining room chairs away from his body. He was a little cold, so I put my coat over him.

I called for an ambulance. We keep the number on top of the telephone table on the first page of our personal phone directory. We have a list of numbers for the police, fire department, our doctor, and some other important services. It was a relief not to have to call information or go through the regular phone directory.

We waited on the floor together. I held his hand and stroked his hair. After a few minutes I remembered that I hadn't called our family physician. I told Bob that I was going to call him and got up to go for the phone. The doctor said that he would meet us at the hospital, which was a relief. I told Bob and he seemed to be more reassured. I think that knowing our own doctor would be there was helpful to him.

When I went back to sit with Bob I remember running out of things to say. So I sang songs, hummed, and kept on stroking his hair and holding his hand. It seemed like hours before the ambulance came, but it was probably no more than fifteen or twenty minutes. I just kept on trying to make one-sided conversation and keep humming.

I don't think Bob knew how scared I was. I didn't really realize either until we got out of the ambulance. I took off my coat in the emergency room and realized that my blouse was soaked with sweat. That was the first really frightening emergency that I ever had to deal with. You hear about people who save others from drowning or bring them back from a heart attack, but you never think that it's going to happen to you.

This story demonstrates well the fact that providing help for someone who is having a stroke does not necessarily mean taking heroic measures. Unless respiration or heart beating has stopped, or there is a sudden lapse into profound shock, basic supportive and reassuring measures are all that is needed until professional help arrives.

First and foremost, it is essential to keep calm. You may feel frightened or alarmed, but as in this case history it is important not to panic. Go to the person who appears to be ill and make a general assessment of their condition. Find out—

1. if they are conscious. You can do this easily by speaking to them in a moderately loud (but calm) voice and by giving them a *gentle* shake.
2. if they can respond to you. This can be through blinking in response to your questions, moving their hands, or other forms of nonverbal communication.
3. if they are breathing. Note whether they appear blue *(cyanotic)* around the mouth, lips, or in the beds of their fingernails. This is a sign of impaired respiratory functioning.
4. if they have a pulse. You can take their pulse at the wrist, at the neck at the angle of the jaw, or in the groin. This will tell you about their cardiac function.
5. if there is an area of obvious bleeding.

If they are conscious and can respond, have a pulse an are breathing, and do not appear to be actively bleeding, you next step is to provide basic comfort and supportive measures Act deliberately, carefully and be reassuring in your manner

1. Position them so that they are comfortable.
2. If the individual is not fully conscious, or seems to be paralyzed, position him on his side. Or, more simply, turn the head to the side. (This measure will help to prevent choking or the aspiration of food or saliva into the lungs.)
3. Loosen clothing, particularly around the neck and waist.
4. If the skin appears cool to the touch, or if the person communicates to you that he is cold, cover him with a blanket or wrap.
5. Prop the head slightly with a pillow, if it makes him more comfortable.

Next, call for emergency assistance. In many commun ties this means an ambulance service, rescue squad, or th police.

Some important things *not* to do.

1. Don't try to lift the person alone. Unless he is in a dangerous or extremely uncomfortable position, wait for help before trying to move him.
2. If he seems to have sustained a head or neck injury, do not move his head. (Don't try to turn the head or prop it with a pillow.)
3. Don't give him any food or water by mouth. This material may be aspirated into the lungs and produce infection or severe damage to the respiratory tract. If surgery is needed upon arrival to the hospital, the presence of food or water in the stomach may increase the risk of administering anesthesia.
4. In general, do not give any drugs, particularly sedatives or pain-killing medicines.

The treatment of the unconscious person who is shock, who suffers respiratory or cardiac arrest, and who ma have profuse bleeding (hemorrhage) requires more advanced measures like cardiopulmonary resuscitation and other life support techniques. These procedures should be learned in a course taught by trained individuals—not from a book. We encourage everyone to take a basic course in emergency care from one of the local groups that we have already mentioned. Fortunately, most people who have a stroke do not suffer these serious emergency complications.

## Reassurance

The importance of reassurance and tender loving care cannot be overemphasized. This involves measures like holding the stroke victim's hand, touching him gently, and speaking reassuringly. If you cannot think of things to say, like the woman in the case history, sing or hum a tune. Long periods of silence can be frightening to the individual who is sick or injured.

It is also helpful to try to communicate *with* the stroke victim. There is perhaps nothing quite so frightening and demoralizing as being unable to make one's thoughts and needs known. Even when individuals cannot talk, they can communicate in nonverbal ways. You can ask the person to blink once to respond affirmatively and twice to respond negatively. You should ask, for instance, "Are you in pain?" If he answers yes by blinking once, then ask, "Do you have pain in your right arm?" In this way you can inquire about the presence or absence of symptoms and take simple steps to provide assistance.

Find out if the person is comfortable. Is he hot or cold? Is his posture and position comfortable? Are clothes too tight or otherwise uncomfortable? Again you can take small measures to make him more comfortable. Do not, however, attempt to lift or move him a great distance on your own. You may produce added injury, aggravate the stroke, or injure yourself. Instead, wait for the emergency rescue team.

Be certain to explain exactly what is happening. Tell him that you have contacted his physician, the hospital, and emergency transportation service. Give him an idea of how soon it will be before help arrives. Keep track of the time by saying things like, "It's been about five minutes since I called. They should be here in another ten minutes or so." A few minutes later say, "It's been about eight minutes now since I called. They'll be here in another seven minutes."

Part of being reassuring is also explaining exactly *what* you are doing *when* you are doing it. Since a stroke may involve paralysis, sensory impairment, and perceptual losses, the person may be unaware that you are providing supportive or comforting measures. Explain all your movements as you perform them. This means, for instance, saying, "I'm going to turn your head slightly to the side." Or, "I'm going to put a pillow under your neck." Ask him to communicate with you about the results of your efforts. Find out, for instance, whether the pillow makes him more comfortable.

Make it clear if you intend to stay with him in the emergency vehicle and in the hospital emergency room. In general, injured or ill persons are fearful of being separated from loved ones during a medical emergency. If you can do so, stay with them until their condition has been evaluated and appropriate medical care has been provided.

These simple supportive measures can make the difference between panic and a sense of calm for the person who is undergoing a stroke in evolution. And, this sense of calm may have a positive effect on the overall mental and physical condition of the stroke victim.

## Emergency Transportation Services

Many people, unfortunately, wait until an emergency actually occurs before they investigate the availability of transportation services in their community. The actual emergency situation is often a difficult time to gather that information and to make necessary arrangements. We encourage you to investigate the services in your area *now,* when you are not in the midst of a potentially stressful situation.

Begin by finding out about the appropriate hospital near you. If you have a personal physician, find out where that person has hospital privileges. There is not much point in being taken to a hospital and then having to be transferred to another institution because your doctor cannot treat you in the first setting. You can avoid this situation by being taken directly to the hospital where your doctor practices.

Next, know where the hospital is and how you are going to get there in the event of an emergency. If you plan on driving, learn the route before the emergency occurs. If you expect to get transportation from a neighbor, friend, or relative, work out the arrangement beforehand.

Certain emergencies are often best handled by persons who have training and experience in the care and transport of the sick and injured. There is always the possibility that improper techniques may further injure the disabled. In general, get professional assistance before attempting to move the person who is having stroke symptoms.

There are a variety of options for emergency transportation. Your choice will depend on local availability, cost, and personal preference. Some of the options are as follows:

1. Private Ambulance Service. These services are provided for a profit. The training of the personnel and the quality of the services delivered will vary in different localities. Some private ambulances will not accept Medicare and Medicaid, or personal checks. Find out about cost and reimbursement requirements before you request their services.

It is also wise to ask them about the training of their personnel. Some services employ individuals who have extremely limited experience and training. Also, find out if they know how to get to your house and to the hospital you wish to go to. And, inquire whether a family member, loved one, or friend can ride in the emergency vehicle. If you are not completely comfortable with the answers to these questions, look for another option.

2. Fire Department Rescue Vehicle. The experience and training of the individuals who provide these services is also highly variable. Often they have American Red Cross certification for basic life support, but lack more advanced training (paramedics have, in general, the most extensive formal training in emergency care). In some communities they may arrive on the scene, but due to local regulations will not be able to transport the stroke victim to the hospital. This will further delay emergency care.

The services provided by rescue vehicles of your local fire department are usually offered for free, or at a minimal cost.

3. Volunteer Ambulance. In many rural areas the volunteer ambulance is the only emergency transportation that is available. The individuals who arrive on the scene may be well meaning, but may have extremely limited training and experience. The service provided may be completely free, or adjusted to individual income needs.

4. Public Professional Ambulance. These services are usually based in a hospital, or they may be provided through a local fire department. For the most part the personnel involved have a high degree of experience and training, particularly if they are paramedics.

The cost of this transportation can be quite high, but is often covered by Medicare, Medicaid, and private insurance. If the hospital receives money from the Hill-Burton Program (a federal program that provides money to hospitals to offset the cost of care to the poor, uninsured, and otherwise needy), they cannot refuse you service because of inability to pay.

A major drawback, however, may be the fact that these services can be overworked. If they have other emergencies, it may take more than a few minutes for them to get to you.

5. Police Vehicles. The level of training and experience in those who respond from the police department will vary depending on the individuals who answer the call. Your request may get a patrol car, or a fully equipped ambulance. If they are involved in other police duties, your call may result in a significant delay.

# What to Take to the Emergency Room

Bring only a few *absolutely* necessary items. Avoid taking cash, extra clothing, books, jewelry, a watch, or other personal possessions. You will have time to bring other items at a later date.

Some things that you should definitely take are—

1. a *Medic Alert* bracelet or other identifying items;
2. your *medications;* the bottles are best, but a list of the medicines including frequency and dose will suffice;
3. proof of medical insurance, such as your Medicare or Medicaid card, Blue Cross card, or other insurance identification.

## At the Hospital

Upon admission to the hospital, you should expect a prompt and thorough assessment of symptoms, and a full explanation of all tests, test results, and costs related to your care. Each of the symptoms should be analyzed by taking a thorough history of the events, performing a complete physical examination, and through the use of a variety of basic laboratory and X-ray tests that may be indicated.

In most cases of a *stroke in evolution,* it will be necessary to admit the individual to the hospital for further evaluation and treatment. While there are, as yet, no proven medical therapies to stop a stroke during the acute phase, hospitalization is necessary for the treatment and prevention of complications that may ensue.

One extremely helpful type of X-ray examination is computerized axial tomography, often abbreviated as the CAT scan or CT scan. It allows for the accurate analysis of cerebral injury, including areas of bleeding and infarction produced by a cerebrovascular accident. Its development over the last decade has enabled physicians, in certain instances, to eliminate other tests such as *arteriography, lumbar puncture (spinal tap), pneumoencephalography,* and the brain scan. These latter examinations are often less precise and sometimes more hazardous than the newer CT scan.

Treatment during the stroke in evolution is designed to monitor the general condition of the affected individual and to prevent complications related to the acute phase. The potential problems include infection, abnormal blood clotting, impairment of the normal heart and respiratory function, and dangerously high or low blood pressure. Once stable, and after neurological deficits no longer appear to be progressing, the rehabilitation program can begin. The work of rehabilitation will be described in the following chapters.

## To Review

1. Dealing effectively with the stroke emergency involves reassurance and an understanding of basic first aid measures. We advise everyone to learn basic life support techniques and the emergency care of the sick and injured. Your local chapter of the American Red Cross, American Heart Association, local hospital, and a variety of community groups provide these training programs.

2. Anyone displaying the symptoms and signs of a stroke should get immediate emergency treatment at a hospital.

3. Transportation to the hospital in the face of an evolving cerebrovascular accident should generally be provided by individuals who are trained to deal with the sick and injured.

4. While waiting for emergency care and transportation— [a.] position the individual in a comfortable manner; [b.] do not try to lift or move him extensively alone; [c.] if the person is unconscious, or shows paralysis of the mouth or throat, turn his head to the side (or turn him on his side) to prevent aspiration of food or saliva; [d.] do not give food or water by mouth; [e.] do not give drugs, particularly sedatives or pain killers.

5. While waiting for the emergency rescue vehicle—[a.] be reassuring; [b.] hold the person's hand and stay with him; [c.] attempt to communicate with him; [d.] describe what you are doing, when you are doing it.

6. Take to the hospital—[a.] your medicines or a list of the drugs you take; [b.] your Medic Alert bracelet or other identifying information; [c.] proof of medical insurance.

# 6

# Rehabilitation

Approximately seventy percent of those who suffer strokes are left with some form of functional disability. Many, perhaps as much as eighty percent, have physical, perceptual, and language deficits that can be helped with modern rehabilitative services. This effort, coupled with psychological and social counseling, can make the difference between dependence on others and an active and independent life-style.

The importance of early and intensive rehabilitation following a stroke cannot be overemphasized. We hope that family members will learn of the potential benefits of modern physical and rehabilitative medicine and insist that their loved ones get these services. The cost, in terms of wasted human potential and years of supportive medical and nursing care, is too high for this treatment not to be offered to stroke victims.

To get an idea of the financial issue, in 1976, the National Survey on Stroke estimated that the annual cost of CVAs was between $6 and $8 billion for the nation. Since that time inflation in the cost of health care and the growth of the elderly population has probably doubled this figure. By 1981, the cost of maintaining a stroke patient in a nursing home was conservatively estimated at $17,000 a year. Successful rehabilitation, where the individual returns to the community, can save up to 90 percent of this figure. There is also a priceless human reward derived from successful rehabilitation that produces independence.

Recent studies indicate that retraining does not necessarily add additional cost to the health care budget. At the Jewish Institute for Geriatric Care (JIGC) a specialized stroke unit was created without adding professional personnel or cost to the institution's budget. It involved reorienting the priorities and daily activities of the facility, but it did not require esoteric technology. Studies indicate that rehabilitation provided by stroke units can make a significant difference when compared to conventional therapy.

The following story, as told by a physical therapist, is an example of what can be accomplished with modern rehabilitation efforts:

> On the stroke unit we make every attempt to treat our patients intensively, hopefully to prepare them for a life of functional independence at home. I can't say that everyone is able to make that kind of recovery, but we still make the effort. Sometimes the surprises and results are incredibly gratifying.
>
> Let me tell you about Mr. Jones who was sixty-three years old when he was transferred to the stroke unit. He had suffered a stroke to the left side of his brain leaving the right side of his body paralyzed. He also was left with an inability to speak that is common to left cerebral injuries.
>
> We were especially concerned because Mr. Jones had a variety of other medical problems: bilateral cataracts, hypertension, and atherosclerotic heart disease. This meant that he had anginal chest pain and rather severely impaired cardiac reserve.
>
> His stroke occurred in the beginning of August and he was sent to an acute care hospital. There, he needed tube feeding and complete care for all his basic needs.
>
> He was one of the first patients on our stroke unit. We realized that he would require many different professional services: physical therapy to improve his strength, coordination, and mobility; occupational therapy to help him relearn to take care of his daily needs; speech therapy to relearn language skills; and psychological counseling. When we first saw him he had a lot of physical problems; for

instance, his face drooped on the right side, he could not move his right arm against the force of gravity, his right hand was not functional, and his right lower extremity was only barely functional. When he tried to walk he would trip because his foot dropped at the ankle.

Our program began extremely intensively. He received physical therapy and occupational therapy four times a day. Each discipline treated him once in the morning and once in the afternoon. The occupational therapy would start early in the morning, helping him to relearn to wash and toilet himself, improve his mobility in the bed and to dress himself. Once he was dressed we would see him in the physical therapy gym and work on his physical strength, coordination, and mobility. In the afternoon he would have occupational therapy in their specialized area and we would work with him in physical therapy on the stroke unit. All our efforts—physical and occupational therapy—were coordinated, so that the specialized exercises in physical therapy would help with his relearning the tasks of daily living in occupational therapy.

Our techniques overlap in many ways that can prove beneficial to the patient. We might employ tapping or vibrational stimulation to muscles in physical therapy sessions, which improve tone in muscle groups that will be retrained by the occupational therapist. The cueing that we do in these sessions also helps with the language training provided by the speech therapist. Our work also helps with motivation, an important aspect of the work carried out by the psychiatrist and social work staff. As you can see, it is all interrelated as part of the total rehabilitation effort.

By four weeks in our institution, he had progressed to the point where he could walk with a four-point cane. Remember that when he came to us he could stand only when supported with aid. At that point, he could walk a hundred feet and climb stairs using the handrail. While he was training we fitted him with an ankle brace and a special shoe that kept his foot from dragging. While we were pleased with his progress, we knew that more progress was still possible.

So, we kept up our rehabilitative efforts. We worked on dressing, transferring, moving from wheelchair to bed, for instance bathroom activities, and walking. By the time he was with us twelve weeks, he could walk two hundred feet, far enough to get along in and around his house. He could dress himself and generally take care of the basic activities of daily living. We discharged him the next week—thirteen weeks after a severe stroke—and he went home. He's been living outside of the institutional setting since. We see him occasionally in the clinic, just to make sure that things are going well. He helped convince us of the importance of the stroke unit.

Sadly, many hospitals and nursing homes provide only cursory and poorly coordinated rehabilitative services. In some cases, they do this primarily to justify reimbursement from the government or private insurers, rather than because rehabilitation is integral to the institution's philosophy. This chapter and the ones that follow will describe the existing technology of rehabilitative medicine and provide guidelines for the expectations of patients and loved ones. If you do not feel that a loved one is getting appropriate stroke rehabilitation, you may wish to seek an institution that is dedicated to this concept.

## The Theory Behind Rehabilitation

In most cases brain cells that are destroyed during a stroke do not repair or regenerate. Nevertheless, neurological function that has been lost can return after a cerebrovascular accident. This is because the brain is adaptive in its structure and function. It can remold its ways of performing vital activities through recruiting new or extending old neurological pathways. This concept suggests that alternative bridges and connections are made that allow the bypass of injured cells and for undamaged centers to take over for areas that no longer function normally.

The theory behind effective rehabilitation is therefore to foster the brain's inherent plastic capabilities. This requires intensive retraining in a variety of areas: movement, balance, perception of space and body, bowel and bladder control, language, and new methods of psychological and emotional adaptation. When taken together these newly learned (or *relearned* may be a better term) functions become the means by which stroke patients work toward independence in the activities and requirements of daily living. It is possible, even in the face of a variety of neurological deficits, to relearn ways to toilet, feed, *ambulate* (walk), communicate, do arithmetic, and perform all the activities of daily living (see chapter 7). These tasks may then be controlled by areas of the brain not previously responsible for these activities.

## The Stroke Unit Concept

Retraining after a stroke involves coordinated efforts by a variety of skilled health practitioners. Unfortunately, after suffering more than a minor cerebrovascular accident, many individuals are sent to nursing homes where rehabilitation services are performed in a suboptimal manner. Three types of shortcomings are often prominent. The efforts of different professionals may be inadequately coordinated. Second, certain highly specialized services such as speech therapy, dentistry, dietetics, *orthotics* (leg braces), and regular occupational therapy, *directed at the specific needs of the stroke patient*, may be entirely absent. And third, there may be inadequate backup services of a psychiatrist or social worker who is skilled in dealing with the psychological needs of the stroke victim.

Unfortunately, there may also be an attitude of pessimism on the part of the professional that is perceived and internalized by the patient. Such an attitude may be an understandable bias based upon a recurring lack of success from inadequately delivered rehabilitation services. Thus, to the health professional, a stroke sufferer may seem to be beyond the help of rehabilitative medicine. As a consequence of this ineffective effort, the stroke patient may never regain optimal functioning.

The modern stroke unit has been designed to overcome these potential problems. Not only do the professionals have special competence, but there is an effort to maintain continuity of care and communication between the different specialists. Individualized goals, based on the type and severity of the cerebral injury and the presence of other medical and psychological factors, are established for each patient on the stroke unit.

# The Stroke Unit Team

Effective rehabilitative efforts involve many professionals who have highly diversified areas of expertise. This is necessary because a cerebrovascular accident commonly produces a variety of deficits: motor, sensory, communicative, spatial, and psychological. It is, therefore, understandable that a stroke victim may require the skills of many or all of the practitioners on the stroke unit team. A modern stroke unit should have services available from the following professionals:

1. Physician. In most cases an individual patient benefits from having a physician who will supervise the overall rehabilitation effort. This person may be a *geriatrician* (a physician who is particularly skilled in the care of the elderly). *Family practitioners* and *internists*, knowledgeable about strokes and rehabilitation, can also provide this supervisory role. In a hospital setting, this physician is often called an attending and is also usually responsible for treating any underlying medical conditions (some of which may have been responsible for causing the stroke). Consulting physicians may be called in by the attending physician in specific areas such as neurology, neurosurgery, infectious diseases, and urology. This approach is common,

since stroke patients may have a number of complicating disorders.

2. Physiatrist. This is a physician who specializes in the evaluation and treatment of physical deficits and who tailors the rehabilitation program to the needs of the individual patient. The physiatrist is usually the coordinator for the physical, occupational, and speech therapy subspecialties, and is knowledgeable about the prescription of assistive devices. Whereas an internist may be board certified (by a professional board exam) in internal medicine a physiatrist would be boarded in physical medicine and rehabilitation.

3. Physical Therapist. The physical therapist works to help restore physical functioning in the disabled and handicapped. They may employ techniques to restore the range of movement of an injured limb. Physical therapists are experienced in the disorders of movement that may result from a cerebrovascular accident.

4. Occupational Therapist. The occupational therapist is skilled in helping disabled persons learn to perform the activities of daily living such as washing, dressing, toileting, eating, taking care of the home, and cooking (see chapter 7). Their efforts complement the work of the physical therapist. He would, for instance, work to train the limited limb to perform activities like grooming and feeding. This is a relearning process that may also involve the use of specialized assistive devices.

5. Speech-Language Pathologist. The speech pathologist, or speech therapist, provides services for restoring the use of impaired language function (see chapter 8). This training involves relearning ways to articulate words, form sentences, explain ideas, write, calculate and understand communication, in general.

6. Psychiatrist. Virtually all individuals who suf-

fer a stroke are victims of debilitating emotions that in varying degrees inhibit their functional recovery. The psychiatrist provides guidance to the patient and the practitioners on the stroke unit in the form of therapy and support for troubling emotions. Effective counseling and intervention to overcome these problems may make the difference between a motivated patient who will recover lost function, and a depressed individual who may never leave the institutional setting (see chapter 9).

7. Social Workers. Social workers carry out therapeutic and supportive counseling in concert with the psychiatrist. In addition, they are often responsible for coordinating family and community support services that may be required to facilitate discharge from the rehabilitation center. Experience has shown that a major factor in the ability of an individual to leave the institutional setting is the availability of adequate social supports. This includes coordinating the efforts of the spouse, other family members, friends, neighbors, visiting nursing, home care services, transportation, nutritional services, and other supports (see chapter 10).

8. Religious Support. It is common for the stroke patient to have fears of dying and to undergo a profound spiritual upheaval as a result of his illness. Clergy, working with the stroke unit team, can provide invaluable support for individuals who feel depressed, unmotivated, or afraid.

9. Dietician. A stroke often produces a variety of complex nutritional needs. There is often, for instance, a period during which only fluid nourishment can be taken. This necessitates a complicated regimen of nutritional support through tube and intravenous feedings. A CVA may produce difficulty with swallowing or chewing and alterations in normal bowel function.

Prolonged bed rest may create a variety of other specialized nutritional needs. The dietician oversees the nutritional support for the stroke patient. The enjoyment taken in food is a basic human need. The dietician and dentist participate in a program to maximize the sensual pleasure derived from food—an essential part of the recovery process.

10. Dentistry. As a result of a stroke many individuals will find that their dentures no longer fit. This is because there is shrinkage of the jawbone and gums, and muscle mass on the paralyzed side. They may also experience a loss of sensation on one side of the mouth producing accumulation of food debris between the gums and cheek. Other new dental problems may also arise such as tooth decay caused by this food debris. Unfortunately for many stroke victims, eating is impaired due to difficulty with chewing or swallowing. The dental profession is actively developing new approaches to the problems and oral disease states of late life. Thus the dentist who treats the stroke patient should be aware of the patient's specialized needs and be able to intervene to prevent added disability to the mouth. The efforts of the dentist may also impact on the ability of the stroke victim to speak intelligibly and to maintain an adequate nutritional intake.

11. Vocational Counseling. A stroke may produce an unplanned and often unpleasant period of retirement. Vocational counseling can assist individuals to return to productive employment. This can be an important adjunct to the motivational support provided by psychological counseling.

12. Nursing. Nursing provides a complex of highly trained professionals: registered nurses, licensed practical nurses, and nurses with specialized training. Their efforts also help create the psy-

chological environment of support, motivation, and encouragement essential for effective rehabilitation.

Some of the specialized functions of stroke rehabilitation nursing are to—

1. establish a bowel and bladder program;
2. promote good sitting posture and balance;
3. help to teach patients to use their wheelchairs;
4. work toward normalizing the patient's life-style;
5. establish daily rest periods;
6. reinforce, assist, and expand upon the training provided by physical, occupational, and speech therapy;
7. provide regular monitoring of the patient's medical condition;
8. administer and monitor the effects of medications and other treatments;
9. provide support and counseling to the patients and their families;
10. prevent complications such as bed sores, injuries due to falls, contractures, infections, and bowel dysfunction.

Particularly important is the bowel and bladder training program, usually carried out by the nursing staff, which provides daily care, support, and motivation. Experience has shown that patients who do not achieve bowel and bladder continence are unlikely to achieve discharge from an institution.

In choosing an appropriate rehabilitation facility for a loved one who has suffered a stroke, it is helpful to inquire about the availability of these different health professionals. Their presence in an institution is an indication that there will be a comprehensive effort at retraining. It is also advisable to inquire about the way in which these professionals work together. Experience indicates that a team approach is likely to produce the most successful rehabilitation. It is generally helpful for there to be one professional, preferably a supervising physician, who knows the family and who will take responsibility for coordinating care.

We should emphasize that a comprehensive plan of stroke rehabilitation does not necessarily require added staff or increase the cost of health care. Many institutions already have these health professionals on staff, or they may exist in the nearby community. It is the coordination of activities—more than the cost—that appears to be most beneficial.

The goal of these efforts is first, and foremost, to restore human potential. We must also remain aware that although successful stroke rehabilitation may seem to be a costly affair, it is in all likelihood far less expensive than years of institutional care.

# Immediate Rehab Efforts

Efforts at rehabilitation should begin as soon as the patient is medically stable. This usually means that the stroke has fully evolved and that there is little danger that movement will produce further complications.

Initial efforts generally involve proper positioning and exercises to prevent additional disability. Hemiplegic individuals, for instance, may tend to lie on their paralyzed side. This can produce bed sores *(decubitus ulcers)* that are painful, disabling and that also may produce serious infections. Bed rest for a prolonged period can be dangerous in other ways; the body may lose its ability to adequately control blood pressure in response to changes in posture, and there is increased risk of developing pneumonia; blood clots may form in the legs, or travel to the lungs. The job of nursing, physical and occupational therapy and ancillary personnel is to initiate early rehabilitative efforts to minimize the risk of further medical complications.

Proper positioning of the limbs, especially during prolonged confinement in bed, is important immediately after the stroke. Flaccidity and loss of pain sensation of an extremity often places the joint in a precarious position and permanent injury may result. In the *lower extremity,* a leg that is allowed to turn outward *(external rotation)* can deform the hip joint, making it impossible for the person to relearn to walk. Even the slight pressure of a blanket or bedsheet may be dangerous to the person with a flaccid lower extremity. It may cause the foot to point downward and may produce a permanent foot drop.

This can be prevented by the use of a blanket cradle that keeps both the blanket and the sheet propped off the foot. A foot board may also be helpful for preventing the flaccid foot from developing contractures of the heel cord *(Achilles tendon)*.

A few general points about *flaccidity* and *spasticity* are worthwhile to mention at this juncture. Flaccidity is an abnormally relaxed, flabby state. In its most extreme state the muscles will have no tone and are incapable of movement under voluntary control (hemiplegia). Be aware that there is a continuum and that muscles may be partially flaccid (hemiparesis).

Spasticity is an abnormally stiff, almost rigid muscular state. The involved muscles are more tense than normal and may move in jerky patterns. Spasticity often develops after a period of flaccidity. When this occurs it can be a *positive* sign, indicating that the affected muscle is getting some degree of neurological signaling.

Different techniques can be employed by the therapist to provide training for flaccid and spastic muscular states. In general, however, prolonged flaccidity is an ominous sign. Recovery of function cannot occur in the face of absent neurological input.

When the *upper extremity* is flaccid there is danger that the shoulder joint may become deformed *(subluxation)*. In this situation the flaccid arm pulls the long bone of the arm *(humerus)* out of its normal position in the shoulder socket. This occurs because a limp and lifeless arm is heavy.

In the immediate aftermath of a stroke, the nursing staff and therapists should position the arm to prevent subluxation. This may require the use of an underarm support while in bed, or in a chair; and at times a sling and bolster that props the arm away from the side.

The arm should also be kept moderately elevated for at least part of the day and during some of the sleeping hours, and it may also be placed in a sling while walking. These strategies are designed to prevent pain, swelling, and permanent postural deformity of the arm and hand.

A set of gentle range of motion exercises should be part of the immediate therapy after a stroke. These exercises move the involved limbs through their normal spatial arcs, loosening the muscles and preventing *contractures* (shortened muscles that prevent the joint from moving through its normal range of motion). This occurs because opposing muscles are not of equal strength. In this struggle, the stronger muscle pulls the joint into a contracted state. Left untreated, a "frozen" joint may result, where the ligaments and joint capsule restrict movement. A typical contracture of the arm deforms it so that it is bent at the elbow. This happens because the biceps muscle that bends the elbow is stronger than the triceps muscle that extends it. The range of motion exercises provided by the nurse and therapist are designed to prevent these disabling contractures.

It is absolutely essential that these range of motion exercises be initially performed by a skilled professional. Overly vigorous or improper manipulation may produce permanent injury to the muscles, tendons, ligaments, or joints. After discharge, family and helpers in the home may participate in a range of motion exercises.

The immediate care of the spastic limb may require splints to prevent contracture. When used on the upper extremity, for instance, they maintain the hand in a posture similar to holding a softball: the wrist is aligned with the forearm and the fingers appear to be grasping the ball. When used on the lower extremity, a support can prevent foot drop or buckling at the knee. Splints and braces are available in a variety of forms and can be used to assist functioning and prevent further disability.

The goal of the *immediate* therapy after a stroke is to prevent additional injury and to pave the way for the concerted efforts of the rehabilitation team. Any prolonged period of inactivity should be avoided, since a variety of complications are likely to result. Once stabilized in the hospital setting, transfer to a rehabilitation center (preferably one with a specialized stroke unit) and additional intensive therapy can proceed.

# The Rehab Plan

The job of the rehabilitation team is to formulate a plan of action. The supervising physician will inform the team of any underlying medical problems that may complicate the rehab effort. The physiatrist will oversee the evaluation of the various disabilities, and the physical, occupational, and speech therapists will perform a detailed analysis of specific functional deficits. Nursing will provide a care plan and a thorough psychological profile will be obtained.

In short, a plan involving all the facets and needs of daily living will be developed. Particular attention should be placed on deficits such as—

1. muscular paralysis (with flaccidity or spasticity);
2. sensory loss (impaired touch, temperature, pain, and position);
3. perceptual losses;
4. areas of neglect or denial;
5. visual deficits;
6. difficulties with balance and coordination;
7. transferring (for example: from bed to chair, chair to toilet and tub, chair to standing);
8. wheelchair mobility;
9. walking, including negotiation of stairs and ramps;
10. problems with feeding (including chewing and swallowing; and food preparation, using tableware, cups, glasses, and plates);
11. hygienic needs like brushing teeth; caring for the skin, hair, and nails; and washing;
12. toileting (including bowel and bladder control);
13. problems with judgment or reasoning;
14. personality control (such as a tendency toward emotional outbursts, or mood swings);
15. depression.

Perceptual deficits and problems with reasoning and judgment are important because they are disabling and potentially dangerous to health and safety. Training in these areas requires a highly structured environment that emphasizes activities performed in a *repetitive* and *sequential* basis. The instruction must be consistent and emphasize concrete ways of performing the simple tasks of movement and daily living (see chapter 7).

A particularly difficult problem in this area is a deficit in the understanding of one's body position in space. This is most common in persons who have suffered a CVA of the right cerebral hemisphere and who also have impairment of functioning on the left side of the body. In this disorder *(anosomaticism)*, they will be unaware of the left side of the body and of objects that exist in the left spatial plane. An example of this is when the person is given a page of print, he will appreciate only material and read words only on the right side. A special form of visial loss may occur for objects on the left side, as well, and there is a *personality* tendency to adopt unrealistic goals and expectations, in general.

The rehab plan must take into account this syndrome of unconscious denial and neglect. Techniques that employ mirrors, visual cues, special exercises, braces, and protective devices may be helpful in this regard. The occupational therapist can use games and devices for training in the needs of daily living, such as dressing and eating, which require effort on the left side. Counseling may be necessary to cope with the problems of impulsive or inappropriate expectations and behavior.

Falls and injuries are common in persons who have *hemineglect*. They should usually be approached from the uninvolved side. Otherwise, you will be approaching from an area of visual deficit and your presence may come as a surprise. In this situation, the person who has had a CVA may turn his head too rapidly and lose his balance. It is helpful for the person with denial/neglect deficits to walk through doorways and hallways wth the involved side closest to the wall or door. This cues the individual to his area of neglect. Also, if he loses his balance, he will have support on the impaired side. However, one must be reminded that injury is possible from bumping into a door or wall.

When transferring to the bed or chair, he must be taught to stand and pivot, bearing his weight on the *aware* (''good'') side, and to sit down carefully, identifying the position of the seat with the aware hand.

When talking to someone with one-sided neglect, it is important to place yourself on the good side. Otherwise, you may be little more than a disembodied and confusing voice. If you are on the neglected or visually impaired side, help him by reminding him to turn his head to place you in view.

The rehabilitation plan should be a stepwise affair in which basic *building blocks* of function are established in a gradual and sequential manner. No single step can be skipped. Progress may seem slow to the patient and family, but it will hopefully move toward the desired goal of independence. Carrying out rehabilitation in this way prevents injuries, future disability, frustration, and the creation of bad habits that can mar progress. A typical plan for therapy usually involves several members of the rehab team working with the patient on the same activity. Nursing, physical therapy, and occupational therapy, for instance, may combine efforts in ambulation training.

The following is an example of a goal-oriented approach to ambulation. Within each set of goals will be a number of steps that must be learned before the next goal can be attempted.

Goal 1. Bed mobility: head control, rolling over, propping up on one arm, moving the legs

Goal 2. Sitting: coming to the sitting position, sitting with help from the therapist, learning to right oneself when moved slightly off balance, strengthening of the hip muscles

Goal 3. Standing: coming to the standing position from sitting, standing with support, shifting one's weight without falling, strengthening of the leg muscles

Goal 4. Ambulation: exercising on the parallel bars, walking with assistance of a helper, walking with assistive devices, and improving distance walked, refinement of gait, negotiating stairs and ramps

The entire process is also an interweaving of physical, sensory, cognitive, perceptual, and mental functions. At the same time that the patient is undergoing training for sitting upright and ambulating, training can be undertaken for the use of a wheelchair. Not every individual will ultimately learn to walk again, but many can achieve independence through the use of a wheelchair. Again, the step-by-step approach is necessary. If the individual cannot achieve independent sitting balance, for instance, it is unlikely that he will be able to use a wheelchair effectively and the rehab goals will need revision.

Wheelchair training is also helpful for improving sensory and perceptual skills and for fostering motivation.

# The Rehab Routine

While every institution will adopt its own schedule of rehab events, any effective program must be extremely *intensive*. At the Jewish Institute for Geriatric Care (JIGC), for instance, most stroke unit patients receive at least four therapy sessions daily. Some activities may be carried out in the patient's room, on the stroke unit floor, or in the specialized areas for physical, occupational, and speech therapy.

The following example from the JIGC demonstrates the importance of an intensive rehab schedule:

Probably every rehabilitation institution can boast of successes that seem to develop in a surprising way. One of ours had to do with a patient who came to us with a number of underlying medical problems that we thought would make it impossible for him to attain functional independence. Yet, because of his persistence and will to get better, and hopefully in part due to our efforts, he was able to go home and return to family life.

When I first saw Mr. Roberts he was seventy-two years old and had suffered from severe cardiac disease for many years. He had triple vessel coronary artery disease, a twenty-year history of diabetes, prior bouts of congestive heart failure, and he was blind in his right eye.

When we first saw him in the stroke unit he was densely aphasic (see chapter 8) and could not make his needs known. He also had lost use of both his right arm and leg, and had developed a painfully subluxed shoulder.

While sitting, he leaned to the right and would often lose his balance. He could not go from sitting to lying on his back without help and could not even roll over on his own. I probably don't have to emphasize this, but he was completely unable to walk.

What worried us was his heart disease. We thought that it might make it impossible for him to work on the physical aspects of his rehabilitation and we were concerned that he might have heart failure or a heart attack while he tried to carry out rehabilitative exercises. It was clear, from our initial evaluation that his program would require the efforts of a group of people: the physician who was skilled in monitoring and caring for his heart condition, the physiatrist who would modify his rehabilitation program in the light of his cardiac needs, and the knowledgeable participation of the physical, occupational, and speech therapists who would have to be conscious of his underlying medical problems. We also had to devise special strategies to account for his one-sided blindness, his dietary needs, aphasia, and so on. He was a rather complicated case, and one that would involve many daily therapy sessions. Throughout his program he had at least four daily demanding sessions of occupational and physical therapy, plus regular speech therapy. Our retraining was conducted under a set of cardiac precautions worked out by the supervising physician. We have a special monitor *(telemetry)*, which allows us to follow the working of the heart while the patient is exercising. When we first practiced basic movements under monitoring, it was thought that he might never progress past the wheelchair level.

Nevertheless, improvement came slowly. After two weeks of intensive therapy, he could get himself from a sitting position to lying down, and could make his wishes known with basic speech. His standing balance also was improving and he could take two steps on the parallel bars. After a month of increasingly intensive work he could tolerate bearing his own weight on his right arm. Remember that this arm had been painful because the shoulder was pulled out of joint. Nevertheless by this time, he could stand independently and walk a few steps with a walker. We had fitted him with a brace that helped to stabilize his foot and leg. After three months in the stroke unit, he was ready to go home. He could stand and transfer himself from a chair to the toilet, and from the bed to a wheelchair. He could walk about seventy-five feet with a four-pointed cane and could negotiate stairs as long as he had a handrail.

I saw him for physical therapy a few days a week over the next four months or so. His heart condition seemed stable and he was able to negotiate around the house. He is still alive three and a half years after his stroke and has never needed to return to the institute as an inpatient. We see him occasionally in the clinic to see how he is doing. I think that we learned from his experience that it is important to proceed with intensive rehabilitation, even in the face of potentially serious underlying medical problems like diabetes or heart disease.

# Rehab Strategies

Over the last thirty years rehabilitative medicine has become a more exacting science with specialized disciplines and areas of controversy. A number of different schools, each describing a particular approach have emerged. In all probability there is no *single* approach that is best for *every* patient and the majority of therapists tend to employ a variety of different strategies at the same time. Nevertheless, understanding the basics of all the approaches provides a clearer picture of the overall rehabilitation process.

The *Bobath* method, developed by Dr. Karel Bobath and Mrs. Berta Bobath, attempts to retrain abnormal *postural patterns* that develop after injury to the brain. Patients will proceed through the training process much like the infant learns to move: beginning with lying prone, followed by moving on all fours, sitting on one's knees, standing, and so on. The goal is to replace abnormal patterns of posture and movement with normal ones by retraining the brain to develop new pathways that replace damaged ones.

Expert handling on the part of the skilled therapist is the basis of the Bobath approach. The patient is moved through the exercises and held and assisted in ways that block abnormal postures and movement. The Bobath method also works toward improving sensory awareness at the same time that it improves muscle tone. The Bobaths felt that it would not be possible to produce normal movement, if posture and the sensation of the body was impaired.

While the Bobaths developed a number of specific techniques, the success of the therapy ultimately depends on the dexterity and feel of the therapist. As one writer commented:

> Handling the patient is comparable to piloting a ship in a crowded harbor or a stormy sea; skill and practice are required, but an exact predetermined course of action is not feasible.... As in handling a ship, the therapist needs to get the feel of the sensitive and responsive instrument (the patient) to know when to block, turn, accelerate, hold steady and to anticipate the reaction.*

The Bobath method also involves individualization of the program for the specific needs of each stroke patient.

The *Brunnstrom* approach was developed by Signe Brunnstrom, who felt that muscles work in specific *groups* and *patterns (synergies)*, which could be harnessed for the retraining process. They are bound in their function by primitive connections in the nervous system that presumably exist on the spinal cord level or at least in centers not controlled by voluntary activity. These muscle synergies become activated after a stroke because the controls normally exerted by the brain are impaired or absent.

In many ways, the conceptualization of recovery after a stroke is similar in the Brunnstrom and Bobath schools. In both, recovery of functioning is seen as analogous to the maturational changes of normal human development. After a stroke, the muscle groups are capable of working only together (in synergy). In the lower extremity, for instance, this means that the hip readily flexes, while the knee and ankle naturally extend (straightening of the leg and downward

---

*Sarah Semans, "The Bobath Concept in Treatment of Neurological Disorders," *American Journal of Physical Medicine*, vol. 46, no. 1 (1967), p. 738.

motion of the foot). In the upper extremity the arm naturally moves next to the body, while the elbow flexes and the forearm *pronates* (turning the palm downward).

The therapist who employs the Brunnstrom approach works to both *facilitate* and *oppose* these natural reflexes. Resistance can be used to spread neurological signals from synergistic muscles to other groups. Skin stimulation can be employed to promote the activity of synergistic muscles.

As spasticity begins to take over from flaccidity the therapist will use a variety of techniques to stimulate reflexes. At the same time stretching exercises will work in *opposition* to the synergies. As spasticity becomes more marked, the basic movement synergies may be performed voluntarily (without stimulation provided by the therapist), even though they may not occur within the normal, full range of motion. As the patient progresses along the Brunnstrom program, movements that deviate from the basic muscle synergies can be accomplished on a voluntary basis. The last step is to coordinate fine movement combinations that are completely independent of synergistic functioning.

An expected sequence of events in the Brunnstrom model would begin by making optimal use of the synergistic movements of the arm and shoulder. These occur in an arc where the shoulder dominates motion, the elbow is kept flexed, the forearm is slightly pronated, and the fingers are flexed. Progress occurs when this posture is broken down, so that the elbow and forearm eventually move freely, and the hand opens. The last stage of repair occurs when nimble movement of each muscle can be performed independently. As was explained earlier, the therapist must work in progressive steps toward this goal—first using the natural synergistic movements of the ''locked'' arm, and making small changes until fine motor coordination results.

*Proprioceptive neuromuscular facilitation (PNF)* is the third important philosophy of physical rehabilitation. Developed at the Kabat-Kaiser Institute in the late 1940s and early 1950s, by Dr. Herman Kabat and his colleagues, the method involves applying resistance to movement and organizing activities in relation to *postural* and *righting reflexes*, which are inherent reflexes. In the cat, for instance, they permit the animal to land on its feet, if it is dropped upside down.

Repetition is extremely important in PNF and efforts are made to keep movement *purposeful*.

As with the Brunnstrom and Bobath approaches, retraining follows patterns that are similar to the normal development of the human infant. In the rehab effort the individual first learns to assume an upright posture and then in a stepwise manner proceeds to ambulation. Attaining upright posture itself involves a sequence of basic steps: rolling, crawling, creeping, kneeling, walking on all fours, then on the knees, and so on. After an upright posture is attained, efforts are initially directed to retrain balance, then to harness reflexes, and finally to work on voluntary movement.

During retraining the therapist focuses special attention on positioning the head and trunk to produce the strongest possible contraction of a muscle. Proper alignment of the head and trunk permits the limbs to function with optimal efficiency. Movement is initially performed in arcs where there is maximal strength, usually those closest to the body. The theory is to employ the stronger parts of the body to stimulate, train, and strengthen areas that may be weakened by the stroke. In general, rehabilitation proceeds from *proximal* areas (those closest to the center of the body) to *distal* ones (the ends of the extremities). Thus, the shoulder movement will be emphasized before movement at the elbow. Once the elbow is functional, work will proceed to the wrists, the fingers, and finally to fine movement of the ends of the fingers.

There are commonalities, as well as differences, in each of these schools. In actuality therapists are practical in their approach and may use elements of each discipline on an individual patient. In the initial evaluation of the person who has had a stroke, and in formulating the treatment plan, the physiatrist and rehabilitation staff will analyze the person's strengths and weaknesses. The individual needs of each client will dictate the approach that is decided upon and flexibility should be maintained to obtain the best outcome.

## Prognosis

It is not possible to predict with complete accuracy the degree of functional return any individual stroke victim will attain. This ultimately depends on the type of deficit, the

xistence of other medical conditions that may complicate
herapy, and the level of motivation that the injured person
rings to the rehabilitation process. There is also the essential
actor of family and community support, which can provide
n enormous catalyst for recovery.

In most cases, if the individual has been offered an
ntensive program, the majority of gains in physical rehabili-
tion will be made within the first 2–3 months. That does not
nean that additional progress will not occur, but that the *bulk*
f the physical recovery will already have occurred by this
me. Improvement then comes from repetition, fine tuning of
bilities, and the continued learning of innovative ways of
erforming the basic tasks of daily living. Recovery of lan-
uage functioning may be somewhat slower.

Flaccidity of an extremity that persists 6–8 weeks after a
troke carries a poor prognosis. On the other hand, if spasticity
; noted within 2–3 weeks of the episode, there is a good
pportunity for recovery of some degree of useful functioning.
his is particularly important for retraining the lower extremi-
y with regard to ambulation. Spasticity of the muscles of the
ip are needed for the individual to begin training for indepen-
ent walking. It is not possible to do this for a completely
accid set of hip muscles.

Excessive spasticity along with an exaggerated tendency
) extend the leg is called an *extensor thrust*. This can be a
erious impediment to relearning ambulation, even though
pasticity has returned to the affected muscles.

The recovery of bowel and bladder control is an impor-
nt sign, at least with regard to the likelihood of the stroke
atient returning home. Individuals who do not attain conti-
ence within six weeks of rehabilitation tend to have a poor
rognosis. Therefore, an intensive bowel and bladder retraining
rogram should be carried out (usually by the nursing staff),
s soon as the individual is medically stable.

The achievement of functional independence within the
onfines of the stroke unit is also an important prognostic
ign. This involves learning independence in transferring
rom the bed to a wheelchair, from the chair to the toilet,
ndependence in wheelchair mobility, and hopefully with
mbulation. Learning to walk independently, however, is not
prerequisite to being able to return home, since indepen-

dence is possible with a wheelchair. It is not surprising, though, that ambulation is often the prognostic sign th stroke victims and families look most to since it is a important *psychological* factor for living independently.

Another important factor for discharge is the maint nance of prior residence during the period of institutionalizatic following a stroke. This is often neglected by the heal system and by the family. The fact is that *one must have home to go to in order to return home*. Individuals who ca maintain their homes during their illness—either with he from the family or social services—have an increased likel hood of becoming independent of institutional life. This is a important argument for providing rent subsidies for low income persons who find themselves hospitalized.

The stroke unit at the Jewish Institute for Geriatric Ca has identified a number of important prognostic factors rela ing to recovery after a stroke. These conclusions should b taken as the experience of an institution that focuses on th rehabilitation of those over age sixty-five and may not b entirely applicable to younger patients. Nevertheless, they a a valuable set of guidelines for stroke patients and familie

Age is, for instance, not an absolute factor preventir recovery. The average age of a stroke patient at the Jewis Institute is seventy-nine. However, older persons may have variety of complicating medical problems in addition to the strokes, and it is these factors that may play a critical rol Illnesses, such as diabetes and heart and lung disease, ofte make rehabilitation more difficult. But they are not necessar ly completely limiting factors. The last case history w presented is a demonstration of this principle.

The experience at the JIGC is that even persons wh have previously suffered amputation or paralysis on the uni volved side can achieve a level of functional independence. addition, heart and lung disease can be treated, as can visual auditory impairment. The point is that *underlying* or *associate medical conditions should be controlled in order to impro the stroke victims' chance for independence*.

The side of the body that has been affected is also n necessarily an absolute limiting factor in predicting rehabilit tion potential. Right cerebral infarcts, which often leave syndrome of denial and neglect for the left side, produce an important complicating factor. These complications can often be overcome with appropriate training.

Left cerebral infarcts may produce language deficits (aphasia). These, too, can be treated with intensive rehabilitation. Probably the most significant limiting factor in this regard is the inability to understand language. These individuals tend to have difficulty during rehabilitation because they do not understand directions (see chapter 8).

Last, there is a prognostic factor that is independent of the stroke sufferer. This is the presence of support systems within the community, including the ability and willingness of the family (spouse and children) to help with the care of the person who has had a stroke. Often this is the single most important factor in determining whether the individual can successfully return home (see chapter 10).

# To Review

1. The majority of individuals who suffer from a stroke will require a comprehensive program of rehabilitative services including speech and language, physical and occupational therapy, counseling, and medical and nursing care. Ideally, such services are provided within a stroke unit where care is taken to coordinate the approach for the optimal result.

2. Effective stroke unit care does not necessarily cost more in terms of dollars or professional effort than other methods of delivering rehab services. In fact, in the long run this type of rehabilitation may be less costly, because it improves the likelihood of attaining discharge from the institutional setting.

3. The human brain is adaptive in its capabilities, so that underused or new neurological pathways can be developed to take over the control of functions lost after a CVA.

4. The rehab program should begin as soon as possible.

5. A flaccid limb is incapable of voluntary movement while a spastic one has increased muscle tone; the latter is a positive sign in the recovery process, since it indicates that neurological signals can reach the involved body part.

6. A bowel and bladder retraining program is an essen-

tial part of the total rehabilitation effort. Experience indicates that individuals who do not achieve bowel and bladder continence are not likely to be capable of returning home.

7. The physical therapist is a university-trained, licensed professional who combines different techniques in a program that is individualized to the needs of the patient.

8. A number of guidelines for predicting the success of the rehabilitation program have been described. Be aware that these are general considerations and that each individual will develop according to his own potential. Prolonged flaccidity is a poor prognostic sign.

9. Both left- and right-sided cerebral injuries can benefit from retraining, although they often require different strategies.

10. One must have a home to go to after the retraining process. We therefore advise that families attempt to maintain their prior residences for a period after the stroke (see chapter 10).

# 7

# Regaining Independence

If you have not suffered a stroke or do not have a disability that makes you dependent upon others, it may be difficult to understand the feelings of someone who has. You can get an idea of their feelings of frustration, helplessness, and depression by trying to perform some of the simple activities of daily living as they do. Try putting on a shirt or brassiere, for instance, using only one hand. If you can do that, then try donning your socks and shoes one-handed. Make sure to pick shoes with laces; if you cannot tie them, think what it would be like never to wear laced shoes. If you are particularly adept as a one-handed person, take a stab at writing a letter with your opposite (nondominant) hand.

It will probably not take long to appreciate the feelings of dependence and loss that arise after a cerebrovascular accident. Usually, once the fear and uncertainty of the immediate events of a stroke have passed, it is the inability to perform the basic tasks of day-to-day living that are of most concern. If you have had a stroke and are reading this book, you probably understand what we are saying. If you have not had a stroke, but are concerned because someone you care about has, this chapter will help you understand how stroke victims overcome deficits.

After a stroke, learning self-care is the most pressing and *personal* of desires. It is the basis by which individuals regain their independence and self-esteem. Self-care tasks are called the *activities of daily living,* often abbreviated as *ADLs*. In most rehabilitation centers ADL retraining is largely the work of the *occupational therapist* or *OT*. At the Jewish Institute for Geriatric Care (JIGC); however, nursing staff also contributes an important role in this endeavor. Like physical therapists, the university-trained and -licensed occupational therapist relies on the plasticity of the human brain. Underutilized and new neurological pathways are trained to take over for cerebral centers that have been damaged by the stroke. Independence is the goal of the ADL program.

# Activities of Daily Living (ADLs)

ADLs are basic self-care tasks: feeding, transferring (for instance, from bed to chair, and from sitting to standing), toileting, bathing, grooming, and dressing. Once the basic simple, but critical activities are mastered, more complicated functions like using the telephone, shopping, cooking, driving a car, and household maintenance can be relearned. Successful recovery of ADLs makes the difference between self-sufficiency and dependence upon others.

What makes OT training different from physical therapy (see chapter 6) is that it focuses on *purposeful activities*. In general, physical therapy (PT) works on basic movements, strength, and coordination, while occupational therapy is geared toward the accomplishment of specific tasks. As one therapist put it, "Occupational therapy is not so interested in wheelchair activity per se, but what one does to get *into* the chair and what one *accomplishes* when in the chair."

In reality, both PT and OT are complimentary. A basic movement may be practiced in physical therapy and then put to use in ADL training. In terms of the modern specialty of rehabilitative medicine, however, it is the occupational therapist who works most directly on the tasks that promote functional independence.

For the person who has had a stroke, mastering ADLs provides a tangible confirmation of recovery. ADLs are, after all, the basic needs that really matter. There is, for example, an incalculable psychological reward in again becoming capable of going to the bathroom on one's own. The other ADLs like washing, dressing, and eating are also intimately related to self-esteem. As gains are achieved, the individual has measurable milestones with which to judge recovery.

ADL training is also a means by which to practice basic movements that restore impaired body parts and to practice language skills being relearned in speech therapy. While it may seem tedious to practice physical therapy exercises, it is less abstract to eat, wash, and toilet oneself. Yet, these activities will improve strength, coordination, range of motion, and the ability to communicate with others.

This work also encourages functional creativity. The stroke victim learns that there are often many alternative ways to compensate for deficits. The disabled must be creative in order to perform the daily tasks that the unimpaired often take for granted.

Progress in ADL retraining is also an important yardstick that helps determine when discharge from the hospital is possible. A timetable of goals can be developed based on the mastery of the tasks necessary to produce independence at home. The following story, as told by an occupational therapist at the Jewish Institute, demonstrates many of the basic principles of ADL retraining. It shows that it is possible to relearn ways to be independent, even in the face of a rather severe stroke.

> Mr. F. is a retired pharmacist who was sixty-eight years old when he had his stroke. When we first saw him in the Department of Occupational Therapy he was paralyzed on his entire right side from a stroke that had happened about three weeks earlier. Since he was right-handed, he found himself completely dependent on our staff for all of his needs. We learned from his wife that their home had a flight of stairs to negotiate, so we took that into consideration in our plan for functional rehabilitation. Despite the fact that he was completely dependent when we first saw him, we formulated goals with the expectation that he would eventually go home and live a relatively independent life.
>
> Our initial efforts involved improving bed mobility. This starts with rolling from side to side, then

sitting up, and lastly transferring to a wheelchair. There are many steps in this process, but within a week or so we had him up at the side of the bed—on his own.

We also prescribed a wheelchair specifically for his needs and instructed him in its use. Even though we work toward the eventual goal of independent walking, the wheelchair is an important aspect of our initial occupational therapy. With the chair he can learn to get into the bathroom, move about for distances that might be too great to handle by foot, and take care of many of his own basic needs.

Our approach is, of course, based on the efforts of a whole stroke unit team. While the nurses were helping him learn to control his bowels and bladder, we were instructing him in toileting. In physical therapy he improved his balance and mobility through the use of a cane, walker, and other assistive devices for ambulation.

While he worked on fine motor coordination, we practiced with him on washing and eating by himself. Our colleagues in the activities department included him in a painting class and regular bingo games.

Mr. F. never regained the use of his right arm. To prevent painful and debilitating disfigurement of his right shoulder we fitted his wheelchair with a lapboard that supported his arm. We also helped him with a sling. Nevertheless he learned to dress himself using certain assistive aids. We replaced the buttons and zippers of his clothes with Velcro and put elastic laces on his shoes. He learned to use a dressing stick and a long-handled shoe and sock donner. Our job in occupational therapy is to help the person become independent. Even if there is paralysis on one side we can do this provided, of course, that the individual has the will to work on ADL training.

Before we discharged him home we made a list of recommended equipment for the house. At the institute we trained him in the use of these devices, but our work would not have been useful if they were not going to be present in the home. The bathroom, for instance, needed grab bars next to the toilet and the tub. He needed a rocker-knife to cut his meat by himself and a *dycem mat* (a plastic pad) to hold the plate from slipping off the table. He learned to shave himself with an electric razor while at the JIGC, but he did not have one at home. We suggested that the family purchase one. Part of the training, you see, involves changing things at home to help people become independent.

We're now three years after his stroke and discharge from our facility. He still lives with his wife. He comes in regularly for his medical appointments to have his blood pressure checked and that sort of thing—but he's still living on his own.

The point of this story is that it is possible to live outside an institutional setting, even after an extensive stroke. In this case, it was possible for ADL training to assist in overcoming paralysis to one side of the body.

# The ADL Program

There is no set pattern of retraining in the activities of daily living that can be applied to all people who suffer strokes. In other words, every program must be individualized to the needs, deficits, and emotional state of the poststroke patient. In Mr. F.'s case, independence was achieved despite the fact that he did not regain functional use of his right side. If he had been able to get the use—even partial use—of his right arm, his program would have been different.

Regardless of the specific deficits that must be overcome, any ADL program must involve a logical progression of steps. It is simply not possible for most people to progress to self-dressing, for instance, before there is mobility in bed. While many patients and families are understandably impatient about what seems to be excruciatingly slow progress, a stepwise approach is necessary to minimize frustration and to prevent injury.

In general, ADL training can begin in the acute care

hospital, as soon as the individual is medically stable. Early efforts at retraining help to prevent unnecessary deformity, loss of strength in the unaffected side, and despondency. Active retraining efforts appear to increase alertness and the motivation necessary for recovery. Taking care of one's own personal hygiene and other ADLs seems to counter some of the apathy and mental lassitude felt after a cerebrovascular accident. For all these reasons, it is advised that both physical and occupational therapy start as soon as possible after the stroke.

As in the case of Mr. F., the ADL program begins with activities performed in bed: rolling over, lifting the hips *(bridging)*, propping oneself up on one arm, using the bedpan and urinal, feeding and washing. These simple tasks are difficult, particularly for individuals who suffer a stroke to their dominant side (that is, right side for the right-handed, and the left side for the left-handed). At first it may be possible to wash only the face or drink using a straw, for instance, because the nondominant side is weak and poorly coordinated. And, in the aftermath of a stroke it is not unusual for there to be some mental confusion that further impairs concentration.

With time and practice, clumsiness diminishes and the unaffected side will compensate and learn to help the affected one. If the right leg is weak or paralyzed, the left leg can be used to move it into the proper position for transferring or dressing. The strong side can also be used to move the weak side through range-of-motion exercises. This will help prevent deformity and swelling.

There are some general rules that are important in the initial stages of ADL training. Individuals should rely predominantly on the strong or *uninvolved* side. Leaning or pivoting on the weak or impaired side of the body may produce injury. In the early stages of retraining, the individual should be *guarded* by another person while transferring or ambulating. In general, it is important not to try to do too much at once, even though it is understandable that some people are impatient to regain independence.

Activities like transferring or ambulating should be performed with grab bars, a locked wheelchair, and safety rails nearby. If support or balance is lost, these devices will help prevent a fall. Remember, after a stroke there is a general tendency for people to be weak and unstable and for there to be perceptual deficits that impair spatial awareness. They may tend to try movements that are not safe. If you are assisting, do not let the person try to do too much; both of you may sustain an injury.

When giving assistance provide only the minimal amount of help that is needed to insure safety and success of the task. Avoid having the individual pull on you. If you doubt your ability to control the activity, ask for another person's help *before* beginning.

Bowel and bladder retraining is an essential part of the ADL program. In general, it can be initiated by nursing and occupational therapy in the early days after the stroke. Along with walking, self-toileting is a basic requirement for independence.

Bowel and bladder training using a urinal and bedpan can begin while the stroke patient is still in bed. The program initially involves getting the person to identify when they need to void and gradually progresses to control of the urge. Even if the person has permanent difficulty with transferring to the toilet, it is possible to learn bed-bound techniques for self-toileting. After successful toileting in bed is achieved, retraining often proceeds to the use of a bedside commode. Last, training can be directed toward toileting in the bathroom.

In the area of personal hygiene, retraining can also begin while the individual is confined to bed. At first a setup of a washcloth, water, and basin should be provided by the nursing or OT staff. Washing can be accomplished with one hand. At first this may be limited to the face. As bed mobility improves, it will be possible to wash the affected arm and torso. When the individual learns transfers, it will be possible to proceed to washing in the bathroom.

A similar stepwise approach is employed in relearning the skills for eating. In most cases, a tray and utensils can be provided while the individual is still in bed. Numerous one-handed eating devices have been developed for assisting with cutting, spooning, and spearing food. There are glasses and cups that have been remodeled for individuals whose grip strength or coordination is impaired. Food can be spooned up against the guardrail that is attached to the side of the plate. A damp washcloth or dycem pad placed under the plate will prevent it from sliding. Specialized cuffs and splints are available to help position or hold utensils.

Limited ADLs can be accomplished by the bedfast person and then expanded when greater mobility is obtained. The basic message is that retraining should begin as early as possible and proceed from the simple tasks to the more complex. When feeding, transferring, toileting, dressing, and washing are mastered, cooking, stair, curb, and ramp mobility, the use of the telephone, writing, and so on can be relearned. Learning ADLs, like PT training, should progress in a highly systematized manner. While many are impatient, attempting to progress too rapidly may produce frustration and injury.

The job of the rehabilitation staff should also be directed at retraining family members who will be in regular contact with the disabled person. They should learn safe methods for helping with transfers, feeding, washing, cooking, and ambulation.

This story exemplifies the comprehensive approach utilized by occupational therapy, which involves family support and the use of assistive devices. The stroke in this case involves a particularly difficult syndrome of denial and neglect, often created by a stroke affecting the right cerebral hemisphere (see chapter 2).

> When Mr. B. came to us he was about three weeks poststroke. When I first met him he was alert and aware of his situation, but he was depressed and unaware of his strengths. We developed a program that would produce improvement through enhancing upon his strength and integrating the use of a variety of assistive aids. We also saw that we could get an important foundation of support and help from his family and worked with them to achieve our goal of discharge.
>
> His stroke had occurred on the right side of his brain and produced a loss of functioning on the left side of his body. What was particularly devastating for him was that he already had a withered right arm from birth. He had learned to compensate for this by using his left arm and hand. When he saw

this side paralyzed, he was terribly depressed. Another problem was that his injury impaired perception of the left side of his body. This is commonly a result of this type of stroke and something that we try very hard to overcome.

From the start, Mr. B.'s goals included feeding and toileting himself. I guess that although he was depressed, he had not given up. He had been living with his brother and knew that if he could feed himself and go to the bathroom on his own, he could return home.

We worked on feeding, washing, dressing, and toileting in stages. Since he was handicapped in the use of both arms, we developed some innovative assistive aids. We attached a loop to the zipper of his pants that enabled him to open and close his fly with his deformed arm. The loop was large enough to allow his thumb to catch it, and long enough to permit him to fully zip and unzip his trousers. We also taught him to use a dressing stick. He learned to feed himself with utensils that were attached to a splint and cuff that were fitted for his right arm. His brother learned to help put on the splint and he could then eat by himself. This part of his body, which had been a burden and embarrassment before the stroke, now took on a new and positive significance.

We also worked on his perceptual disorder. When I first saw him he had little awareness of his left arm and side. I would often position myself so that he would have to rotate his head to see me. Sometimes we would work with puzzles and games and I would put pieces into the space of his neglect. He learned to be aware of this problem and to compensate for it.

We also worked on his desire to become independent. The assistive devices, like the splint for eating and the dressing stick, do not make people independent by themselves. These devices become assistive only through the retraining process and individuals learn a general psychology of constant adaptation. Mr. B. did exceptionally well in this regard and was creative in his ways of performing his self-care.

Eventually he went home to live with his brother. The assistive devices were helpful, and we arranged for home safety equipment to be installed and for regular visits from a home health aide. Mr. B. may be disabled, but he is not dependent.

Mr. B.'s story is gratifying for a number of reasons. First is that the denial and neglect syndrome is a particularly difficult and frustrating problem to overcome after a stroke. In addition, he came to the rehab process with the additional problem of a withered arm. Nevertheless, he and his brother learned ways of compensating and have been able to live independent lives.

## Assistive Devices

The occupational therapist is skilled in the design and use of assistive devices that can help the disabled stroke victim overcome a variety of functional deficits. Some aids are commonplace objects put to new use, like a damp washcloth placed under the plate at the dinner table. Other devices are more complicated and may be prescribed by a physiatrist, purchased from a surgical supply outlet, or custom-made by the occupational therapist.

Learning to use these aids is a cornerstone of the retraining process. For Mr. B., the adaptation of his clothing made independence in dressing and toileting possible. It is important to emphasize, however, that assistive devices do not move or activate themselves. The disabled person must *learn* to employ them in constructive activities of daily living. This is the specialty training provided by the skilled occupational therapist and physiatrist.

In many cases the assistive devices are essential for *safety*. Grab bars placed next to the toilet and in the bathtub fall into this category. The bars facilitate transfers and make the process safe. Unfortunately, aids that primarily increase safety in ADLs are often not covered by Medicaid, Medicare, and private insurers. This policy seems shortsighted, since any device that offers independence through improved safety is likely to be far less expensive than the cost of long-term institutionalization.

If you feel an assistive device is needed in your home, find out whether it can be paid for by your existing insurance *before* purchasing it. Sometimes the aid will be covered, if they are prescribed by a physician. Your medical provider, occupational therapist, or social service personnel of a rehab facility should be knowledgeable about reimbursement practices.

Many assistive devices must be properly fitted or tailored to the needs of the disabled person. Inappropriate devices are not only a waste of money, but they can be a source of frustration and injury. In general, we suggest that you have these devices prescribed by a professional and that you do some comparative shopping before buying. Prices and services vary significantly (see chapter 10).

# Bed Mobility

Bed mobility is the basis for the ADLs like feeding, toileting, washing, and dressing. It reduces the likelihood of developing painful and dangerous pressure sores and is the foundation for the rest of the retraining process.

Sitting in bed can be made more comfortable by following a few simple guidelines. First, weight should be distributed evenly on both hips and the head should be in an upright position between the shoulders. A small rolled towel can be placed under the small of the back to maintain the normal lumbar curvature. If there is weakness or paralysis of the upper extremity, supporting the arm on a pillow, bed table, or in a sling will help prevent pain and deformity.

Care must be taken to progress with slow and deliberate movements in the first days after a CVA. Sudden changes in blood pressure may produce light-headedness or loss of consciousness. Attempting to move too rapidly may produce injury to weakened parts of the body.

1. At home the bed should be arranged so that the height is comfortable for the person to sit with

the feet on the floor. For most people this is
about eighteen to twenty inches from the floor
level.

2. The bed should not move during transfers. Remove roll about casters and wheels and place
rubber pads or wooden blocks under the legs.
Putting the bed in a corner may also be helpful.

3. Use a firm mattress or place a plywood board
between the mattress and box spring.

4. Arrange the bed so that the person's strong side
is on the free side of the bed when lying down.

5. A blanket cradle may be needed to keep the
covers off the feet (see chapter 6).

Proper positioning of the bed will be a significant factor
for facilitating safe and effective movement in bed and for
transferring in and out of bed.

## Transfers

As progress in bed mobility is achieved, the ADL
retraining program usually places greater emphasis on transferring from bed to wheelchair, from wheelchair to bed or to other
seats, and to and from the toilet, and turning the wheelchair.

Wheelchair transfers are an important milestone in regaining
independence. For many the wheelchair may be needed to
replace ambulation—at least for covering significant distances.
It is, therefore, essential to be able to get in and out of a chair
by oneself, if independence is to be realized.

The rehabilitation staff will emphasize this portion of the
retraining process, even when the goal of independent ambulation
is expected. Some important points to be aware of when
helping with transfers are as follows:

1. Provide only the minimal amount of assistance
that is needed to insure a safe transfer.

2. Before beginning the process make certain that
the brakes of the chair are locked and that the
footrests are lifted or moved out of the way.

3. Clear the immediate area of any object that may
be a hindrance.

4. Know where you want to go and how you are going to get there before starting.
5. Have the disabled person move in the direction of the strong side.
6. Don't let the person pull on you. Stand in front of him and assist by placing your arms under his. Only if there is no danger of falling should you place yourself on the weak side during the transfer process.
7. Perform the transfer slowly and deliberately.

You can help to avoid back strain by relying primarily on the muscles of your arms and legs. If you sense a problem or feel apprehensive, *stop* the transfer and rest before starting up again. Take a few moments to go over the transfer routine. And, if you have any hesitation about your dual ability to perform the task, get additional help from another person.

The disabled person's strong arm should be kept free to assist with the transfer activity. When going from the bed to a chair, the strong arm should support the process by holding onto and pushing off the side of the bed. The left hand should move to the left armrest of the wheelchair, for a person with right-sided weakness or paralysis, and he should pivot on his left leg. Reverse this process when there is a left-sided deficit. Remember, safe transfers depend primarily on the strength and coordination of the person who has had the stroke. You are there to provide guarding and assistance, but should not expect to carry out the entire burden of the activity.

To facilitate transferring, the chair (or wheelchair) should be at the appropriate angle to the bed. For a person with right-sided weakness the seat should face the foot of the bed and the chair's backrest should point toward the head of the bed. The chair should be at an angle of about 15 degrees to the side of the bed. When getting *into* the bed from a chair reverse the entire setup by 180 degrees. The seat should face the head of the bed at an angle of approximately 15 degrees.

When moving onto the toilet from a wheelchair it is helpful to have a grab bar for support. For an individual with right-sided weakness (a strong left side), the grab bar should be located to the left of the toilet. Before transferring, the wheelchair should be placed facing the toilet. The person stands up with the aid of the left armrest of the wheelchair, reaches over to the grab bar, pivots and gets into position for slowly moving onto the toilet. The point we wish to emphasize is that the strong side should also be employed to assist and guide the transfer process.

Part of the retraining for independence should include instruction in transferring into and out of an automobile. In general, the principle is similar to that for other transfers. The window of the car should be rolled down completely so that the door can be used for support. Family and friends can help by placing the vehicle close to the curb and by seeing that the window is rolled down to help support a safe transfer.

## Wheelchair Mobility

Learning to use a wheelchair is another essential aspect of regaining independence. The occupational therapist, along with professional nursing and physical therapy, will design a program to include the following basic elements:

1. Individuals must learn how to propel the chair, including the coordination of legs and arms. Chairs can be propelled with one hand and in the face of more severe disability can be propelled electrically.
2. Individual adaptation of the chair is necessary to meet the needs of the person who is disabled. The proper chair must be chosen, its height adjusted, and all fittings tailored to the needs of the person who will use it. The chair can be fitted with a commode and clips with which to attach personal items.
3. For individuals with perceptual problems the chair can be fitted with a clear Plexiglas armboard.
4. Both the person who uses the chair and significant others (family and close friends) should know how to check the brakes, seat, back, and other moving parts on a routine basis.
5. Padding can be put on the back or on the seat to

insure comfort and to prevent the development of pressure sores.
6. Instruction should include proper sitting posture while in the chair.
7. The house and immediate environs should be adapted to make for safe use of the wheelchair. Thresholds should be removed from doorways; scatter rugs should be removed from floors; and ramps should be installed alongside steps.

The wheelchair has undergone major improvement as an assistive device over the last thirty years. Modern chairs can be adapted for almost any home or use. They are much lighter than they previously were and can be collapsed conveniently. Getting the correct wheelchair for your needs usually requires careful prescription by the rehabilitation team. Before leaving the rehab facility, family, close friends, and the person who has had a stroke should become thoroughly versed in all aspects of wheelchair mobility and maintenance.

# Ambulation

Next to toileting, disabled individuals often consider ambulation (walking) their most desired goal. Getting back on one's feet has psychological, as well as practical, benefits. Unsteady ambulation, however, is a major cause of injury and disability. Older persons in general, and certainly those who have had a stroke, are at high risk for sustaining falls.

Safe ambulation requires intensive retraining and attention to many small things that we may take for granted. There are often specialized needs for footwear, for instance. Some people rely on sneakers, but may have difficulty if they need added lateral support. Or, they may pad around the house in slippers that have slippery soles. Part of the work should be to help suggest the appropriate shoes for safe ambulation.

Safe ambulation also involves overcoming perceptual deficits that may persist after a stroke (see also chapter 2). Some people are left with areas of visual deficit. They may tend to trip or bump into things. Since strokes commonly affect older person, there may be other visual problems, as well. It is important to ambulate with the help of appropriate corrective lenses and in areas that are well lit.

Before attempting to ambulate at home, make certain that the house is made safe for this purpose. Remove all scatter rugs and get rid of any unsteady furniture. It is helpful to have night lights scattered throughout the household, particularly in the hallways, stairs, and bathroom. A night light can be placed in the outlet for the electric razor in the medicine cabinet, for instance. You can add handrails to the hallways and other areas where there may be nothing to help support the person in a moment of unsteadiness.

The point is that not only must the person who has had a stroke be retrained in ambulation, but the environment must be altered to facilitate this activity. An important job of the rehab staff is to instruct families in ways to make the home safe for walking.

Yet another aspect of the ambulation program is training in the proper use of a walker or cane. Acceptance of the need for these devices is also critical, since they are sometimes considered an unwelcome reminder of disability. Too frequently a disabled person will deny that they need an assistive device for ambulation. They may attempt to walk without their cane, for instance, and sustain a dangerous fall.

A cane or walker must be fitted by a skilled rehab specialist. The proper height for a cane or walker allows the person's elbow to be bent slightly when it touches the ground. The cane should be held in the *strong arm* and used in tandem with movement of the weak leg. The weak leg should not precede the cane while taking a step. There is a good chance that the weak side will give out and the individual will fall.

For the most part, short steps are safer than large ones. The safest method involves placing the cane a few inches ahead of the strong foot and bringing the weak leg to it. One's body weight should be fairly evenly distributed between the weak leg and the assistive device.

Wide-based canes are extremely helpful for individuals who may be unsteady. Some have four points for legs and nonskid rubber bottoms. The new canes are light and some can be folded for travel.

When negotiating stairs it is usually helpful to suspend or hang the cane from a pocket or arm. Use the handrail for support and go up with the *strong* leg leading the way. Bring the weak leg to the same step and then move the strong leg to the next tread. Fit your home with a handrail on both sides of the stairs, or if this is not possible place one railing down the middle of the stairs.

Going *down* stairs employs the opposite strategy. Lead with the weaker leg, keeping body weight primarily on the strong limb. Use the handrail for support and hold onto it with the strong side. Once the weak leg is securely on the step below, gradually bring your strong leg down to it. Remember, your household's stairs should be fitted with nonskid treads. Curbs should be negotiated as though they were a single step and the cane used for support in place of the handrail.

# Feeding

A variety of strategies and assistive devices have been developed to help the hemiplegic or hemiparetic person eat with one hand. The simplest approach involves spooning or spearing bite-size pieces. Assistive devices, such as a wrist splint, can help handicapped persons get food into their mouths. Cups and glasses are available that have been remodeled to help the strength and coordination of persons with limited grasp.

In order to eat with one hand the food plate must be stabilized on the table. As already mentioned, a damp wash-cloth placed under the plate will prevent the dish from slipping. A plastic pad (dycem), which similarly anchors the plate, can be left permanently on the table.

A plate guard can be clipped to the side of the plate. Food can then be pushed against the guardrail and scooped onto the eating utensil with one hand. A swivel spork, which combines the tines of a fork, the bowl of a spoon, and a swivel handle keeps the utensil level if the wrist is disabled. A rocker-knife that has a sharpened curved edge can be employed to cut food with one hand. This device works by substituting rocking action for the usual sawing action of a knife.

In general, if the grasp is weak or if movements are unsteady or tremulous, it may be helpful to use eating utensils that have short, fat handles. The handles of most eating utensils can be widened with sponge rubber or a washcloth. It is also possible to purchase implements already manufactured in this way. If movements are jerky, the utensil can be covered with plastisol to prevent injury to the mouth and teeth.

Some individuals may find self-feeding difficult because of poor coordination, weakness, or a limited range of motion of the wrist. Mr. B. in our last case history had such a problem because his arm had been withered from birth. In this situation, a wrist support may be employed to keep the hand in the proper position for feeding. A universal cuff can also be employed. This device has a pocket that holds the eating utensil in such a way that a weak hand grip is overcome. Some assistance is usually required to put the cuff on, but once in place helps promote independence in feeding.

There are a variety of specially constructed cups and glasses that assist in drinking, including those fitted with T-shaped or elongated handles. They can also be fitted with covers and spouts that prevent spilling. It is important to be particularly careful when drinking hot liquids. Hot coffee, for instance, if spilled into the lap can produce a significant burn. Assistive devices for feeding also may provide an important safety function.

Two simple aids should be noted with regard to drinking. Most liquids can be sipped through a straw and the majority of individuals who have had a stroke can drink independently using this simple technique. And a terry cloth coaster or washcloth can be used to help prevent cups and glasses from spilling.

There are a great many assistive devices for feeding. There are sandwich holders, a spike board to help with one-handed bread buttering and cutting, special can openers, and an extensive list found in most surgical supply catalogs. Training in the use of these devices should be part of the stroke rehabilitation program. They can make a significant contribution in the effort to regain independence.

Maintaining a proper diet after a stroke is an essential part of the rehabilitation program. While the basic principles of a balanced meal plan apply as before, there are often some special considerations created by the stroke. First, while there is a continued need for vitamins, minerals, protein, carbohydrate, and fat, there may be a *reduced* total caloric need. This occurs when the stroke inhibits activity. It is therefore necessary for the individual to get the same basic nutrients from a smaller overall amount of food. Limiting the intake of foods that are high in "empty calories" like candy, desserts, and fatty meats are helpful in this regard.

Second, there is an almost universal tendency toward constipation. Bed rest and the neurological effects of the CVA make the bowel sluggish. Foods that contain large amounts of fiber, particularly bran and whole grains, will promote normal elimination. Adequate food intake will also be beneficial.

Third, there may be an altered sensation of tastes. Foods that were previously enjoyed may now seem unpalatable; or the person may not be able to chew and swallow foods that were usually part of their diet. A new selection of foods may be needed to promote adequate nutritional intake in the face of these changes. Changes in dentures and other dental work may be needed to aid with chewing and swallowing.

The point is that the services of a dietician may be essential in the recovery process. The taste, nutritional composition, and texture of food can and should be altered to accommodate the needs of the stroke victim.

# Toileting

Once the individual can recognize and control the urge to void and defecate, and after the appropriate transfers have been learned, it is possible for toileting to be performed in the bathroom. For many, this intimate activity can be performed independently, if proper assistive aids have been installed in the bathroom.

Essential to this end is the installation of a grab bar on the wall next to the toilet. There is also available a set of two bars that attaches to the toilet seat. A large ring that elevates the toilet seat further aids transfers by allowing the individual to remain semiupright (rather than squatting) on the toilet. The toilet paper should be mounted within easy reach. A bidet can also assist in the cleansing process. There are bidet-type attachments available for the standard toilet.

Dressing and undressing for toileting is frequently difficult after a stroke. Wearing suspenders or attaching pants to the shirt by buttons can help raise trousers and prevent injuries, which can occur when the person bends over to pick up his pants. So, clothes should be modified with suspenders or attachments, or purchased with special modifications through catalogs for handicapped persons. A dressing stick kept by the toilet can also be used.

It is essential for the person who has had the CVA to leave added time for performing transferring and undressing prior to toileting. This will prevent embarrassing accidents. Velcro-modified zippers, clasps, and buttons can also facilitate the speed and efficiency of dressing.

# Dressing

One-handed dressing is possible, but it takes intensive retraining in the rehabilitation setting. It is another one of the intimate activities that is necessary for regaining self-esteem, as well as independence.

There are many assistive aids that can help with one-handed dressing: sock and shoe donner, dressing stick, Velcro substitutes, and elastic laces. Some general principles are important to note.

1. Clothing should fit loosely.
2. Avoid excessively baggy garments that may get caught in doors, knock over household objects, or be an impediment to ambulation.
3. Closures should be in the front of the garment, rather than on the back or sides.
4. If balance is steady, it is easier to dress at the side of the bed, rather than in a wheelchair.
5. Shirts, coats, and dresses should first be put *on* the weak arm and then pulled behind the body. The uninvolved side can then be maneuvered into the garment. Take the garment *off* of the weak side first, and then shake it from the strong side.
6. Pants should be put onto the weak leg first. Cross the weak leg over the strong one and pull

the pants on. Next put the pants over the strong side. If there is *any* uncertainty about standing balance, pull the pants over the waist while lying in bed. It is possible to do this by lifting the pelvis off the bed and simultaneously pulling the pants up. A shifting side to side motion can be used if it is difficult to lift the pelvis and pull up the trousers simultaneously. When taking the pants off, remove them from the strong leg first.

Special attention should also be placed on one-handed dressing with shoes, socks, and brassieres. Home closets can be renovated to make clothing readily accessible from a wheelchair. And, it is worthwhile to emphasize that appropriate clothing does not necessarily have to be unstylish. Part of the rehabilitation process is to regain self-esteem, as well as normal functioning.

# Personal Hygiene

ADL retraining for washing and grooming can begin in bed during the early days after a cerebrovascular accident. At first this may mean washing only the face. When bed mobility and sitting balance improves, it may be possible to wash more of the body. Once wheelchair movement and transfers are mastered, washing and grooming can be performed in the bathroom. But, be aware of the fact that the bathroom is probably the most dangerous area in the house for the person who has had a stroke. Injuries often occur—

1. during transferring from wheelchair to toilet or tub;
2. while putting on, taking off, or adjusting clothing;
3. because the individual's body is wet and soapy;
4. when surfaces like an enameled tub or sink, or tiled walls are wet and soapy;
5. because steam impairs vision or fogs glasses;
6. because immersion in hot water produces a sudden drop in blood pressure and fainting or loss of balance.

The bathroom must be made safe for the person who has had a stroke. There are a number of assistive devices that facilitate washing and grooming activities. Grab bars and a tub seat are virtually indispensable. The tub seat may be designed in a variety of ways; it may sit in the tub or straddle the edge. A board may be helpful to assist in transferring from the wheelchair to the tub seat. We suggest that you work out the redesign of the bathroom facility with the help of the rehabilitation staff. Do this before the individual is discharged home.

It is often difficult for the stroke victim to wash the uninvolved (unaffected) upper extremity. A brush that clamps or adheres to the sink or tub with section cups will help with this activity; the hand and arm can then be scrubbed against this brush.

A hand-held shower nozzle is another helpful and relatively common adaptive aid. Soap may be tied to a string and then tied to the neck or attached to the tub. Since wet soap is slippery, you will need the string to retrieve it if it is dropped. You can buy soap that is manufactured in this manner, or make your own by placing a hole in the bar.

If grasp is limited, a sponge stick may be useful. This simple device also assists in washing the feet and back. A terry cloth bath mitt can be used when grip is impaired. If towel drying is difficult, it may be simpler to put on a terry cloth bathrobe.

Sometimes a stroke impairs temperature discrimination. This sensation may be further diminished in individuals who have diabetes. It is, therefore, a good idea to have an unbreakable plastic thermometer next to the tub and sink for testing bath water. In general, it is unnecessary to bathe in water that is hotter than 100 to 110 degrees F. (38–43 degrees C.).

Nonskid bath mats should be placed in the tub and alongside it. They should be changed regularly since the suction cups wear out. A nonskid mat that loses its ability to adhere firmly to the tub or floor is an *extremely dangerous* item—the unsuspecting individual expects to be safe on the mat and suddenly sustains a serious fall.

In most cases it is safer to take a bath than a shower. Hair can be washed in the bath with the hand-held shower nozzle. If you do not have a tub, it is possible to place a seat in the shower and to use the hand-held shower nozzle.

Oral hygiene is another essential part of stroke rehabilitation. Some people have impaired muscular activity of the face and mouth after a CVA. This may hinder the normal process by which food is cleaned from the mouth after a meal. Part of the retraining activity is to help individuals become aware that food has pooled in the mouth. A thorough dental evaluation should also be part of the stroke rehabilitation program.

One-handed brushing is not much different from the oral hygiene habits most individuals practice. There are special problems, however, for people who have dentures. A brush can be attached to the side of the sink to facilitate one-handed cleaning of dentures. Take care to fill the sink about halfway with water prior to cleaning. If the dentures drop into the sink, the water will help prevent them from shattering.

A water pic is a simple and relatively inexpensive assistive device used to clean the mouth and teeth for anyone left with limited range of motion or strength. There is also a sling-shotlike device for one-handed flossing.

Hair grooming may pose special problems when the uninvolved side has limited range of motion. Extension handles are available to help the arm and hand get behind the head. Weighted cuffs for the wrist may help stabilize the hand and produce more accurate hair grooming when movements are jerky or tremulous. In general, a comb or brush with a large handle will be easier to use than one with a small handle.

Both men and women should use an electric razor to shave. Many electric razors have a rechargeable battery and can be used independently from an electric outlet. They are generally small, lightweight, and easy to handle.

In most cases, women who have sufficient coordination to feed themselves can become adept at the use of cosmetics. As with the comb and brush, the larger the handle on the cosmetic, the easier it will be to use accurately. An emery board attached to a table or cutting board facilitates paring of fingernails.

After a stroke most persons should have regular foot and toenail care from a podiatrist. This will prevent injury or deformity from poorly coordinated efforts at nail care. Shoes should be fitted to prevent unnecessary calluses, bunions, and other deformities.

# Driving

Relearning to drive is, for many, like relearning to walk. It is perceived as an essential physical, emotional, and social part of the recovery process. However, since driving may be dangerous after a stroke, careful retraining and evaluation should be performed before returning behind the wheel.

There are many schools that specialize in, or include, driver training for handicapped persons. It is advised that anyone who has suffered a stroke attend one of these programs and obtain a thorough evaluation of their driving skills. This includes an analysis of any potential areas of perceptual deficit, as well as difficulty managing the motor aspects of driving.

In addition, the automobile can be adapted to the needs of the handicapped individual. This includes changing the way in which the vehicle is driven (hand and foot controls), handicapped license plates, and modification to handle improved wheelchair access. Remember, assistive devices do not drive a car. In particular, they cannot overcome perceptual deficits that impair the awareness of other cars, areas of vision, and road hazards. Before returning to the automobile, have a full evaluation of stroke-related limitations and a consultation with your medical provider. In some states, clearance from a medical professional is required before the individual is again allowed to drive under existing state law. Most persons, however, who have sustained a mild to moderate disability from a stroke, and who had driven prior to that stroke, will be able to drive again. Those persons who have visual or perceptual losses will probably not drive. In all cases it is advisable to inform the insurance company that provides coverage that the driver has a disability.

# Sexuality

It is normal to have sexual desires after a stroke. Nevertheless, the episode may produce serious handicaps to returning to normal sexual activity. There may be changes in physical appearance that require adaptation on the part of one's partner. And, there are commonly physical and sensory limitations that may alter the way in which sexual relations are performed.

Most individuals who are capable of bowel and bladder control and ambulating will also be physically capable of resuming sexual activity. The decision of whether to have sex will depend on the emotional adjustment to the stroke. If sexuality appears to be a problem, it is important to discuss the issues with a knowledgeable professional. Unfortunately, many lay and professional individuals have mistaken notions about sex after illness and injury. Get advice and counseling from a professional who has experience in the field of rehabilitative medicine.

A few misconceptions, however, should be dispelled. First, is that sexual activity and orgasm are not likely to produce another stroke episode. Secondly, there are many alternatives to sexual intercourse, as a means of deriving satisfaction. Kissing, hugging, mutual masturbation, and oral sex are activities that can lead to satisfaction without participating in intercourse. And, there are many positions to have intercourse that can compensate for physical disability. Third, it is important to be aware of the uncertainty that handicapped persons have about resuming sex. They may feel unsure of their ability to satisfy their partner and about their appearance. They may have sexual feelings, but think that it is inappropriate to express them. For these reasons, and for other considerations that may apply to individual family situations, it is important to discuss the issue of sex with your medical practitioner and a qualified counselor.

# The Optimistic View

We have provided a brief overview of the concepts and possibilities created by modern occupational therapy. The strategies and assistive devices that have been described are but a small part of the complete effort toward regaining independence. Our point is that this is a realistic goal for a great many individuals who suffer a stroke. Everyone who suffers a CVA deserves an intensive effort at rehabilitation and many who were previously considered beyond help can now see a brighter future.

The American Heart Association has a variety of pamphlets that describe devices and strategies helpful for regaining independence. One such booklet, *Up and Around*, by Dr. Florence Mahoney and Dorothea Barthel, B.A., P.T., is helpful for its description of some of the basic activities of daily living. There are many catalogs provided by surgical supply companies and through Sears Roebuck that list assistive devices. Most importantly, use the guidance of the occupational therapist and other professionals on the stroke unit team to develop strategies for regaining independence after a stroke.

# To Review

1. The activities of daily living (ADLs), like feeding, washing, grooming, transferring, toileting, and dressing, are the basic activities that produce independence and improved self-esteem.

2. Progress in ADLs can be accomplished in the face of many deficits including limitation of the uninvolved side of the body, perceptual deficits, and language problems. An intensive program in ADLs also fosters improvement in other aspects of the rehabilitation program.

3. Learning self-toileting is an extremely personal part of the ADL program. It can begin in bed and proceed in stages through the rehabilitation program. Experience shows that self-toileting is an essential activity for most people who wish to attain discharge from the rehabilitation facility.

4. The bathroom is a potentially dangerous part of the house. Grab bars, adequate lighting, and a variety of assistive devices are necessary in order to enable stroke victims with deficits to be able to negotiate the bathroom safely. Discuss the appropriate alteration of your home, and particularly the bathroom, with the rehab staff before contemplating discharge.

5. A modern professional ADL program should begin, as soon as the stroke victim is medically stable. Improvement in ADLs is an important factor for enhancing motivation in the total recovery process.

6. Don't buy assistive aids or safety equipment before checking with the professional rehabilitation staff. These

devices should be tailored to the individual needs of the handicapped person.

7. Get medical clearance before returning to driving. Consult with your state motor vehicle department concerning regulations for handicapped persons.

8. Sexuality is a normal part of living. Most individuals who can ambulate and control bowel and bladder functions can resume sexual relations. Counseling may be helpful to assist in the transition to a resumption of sexual relations.

# 8

# Relearning Communication

The ability to speak, read, write, and use complex language, in general, is a uniquely human activity. The loss of this capacity in the aftermath of a stroke is a major blow to the essence of one's being: self-esteem, independence, relationships with others, ability to earn a livelihood, and the accomplishment of even the simplest of tasks. Retraining to use communicative functions is, therefore, an essential part of a stroke rehabilitation program.

The *speech-language pathologist*, sometimes called the *speech therapist*, is a university-trained and licensed professional who specializes in training the handicapped in the area of language and communication. These health professionals work in a variety of settings including public and private schools, hospitals, rehabilitation centers, skilled nursing facilities, community clinics, and in private practice. They may conduct therapeutic sessions in any one of these institutions or in the patient's home.

Training to overcome speech and language deficits should begin early in the rehabilitation process. Positive results provide important emotional reinforcement and support that frequently enhances other rehab efforts. Gains made in communicating have the immediate advantage of helping with medical and nursing treatments and in the work of the physical and occupational therapists.

# Aphasia

Deficits in the understanding and use of language are described under the general medical term *aphasia*. Commonly, individuals suffer from a partial loss of language function and deficits may vary from mild to severe. An individual may, for instance, be capable of using a single word or simple phrase, but be unable to form complete sentences. Or, he might understand simple primer-level words, like *chair* and *stop*, but become confused with more complex conversation. Others may be capable of understanding speech, in general, but be incapable of reading and understanding telephone conversation.

Over the last century medical scientists have determined that the human brain contains geographically specialized and distinct areas that control different communicative functions. There are specific regions for the *production* of language (speaking, writing, and gesturing) and yet different areas for the *reception* of information (comprehending the spoken word, reading, and appreciating the gestures of others). There are separate portions of the brain that control the eye movements needed for reading and for seeing the movements of others; and still other areas for coordinating the muscles of respiration, the mouth, lips, tongue, and vocal cords involved in the production of speech. Weakness, paralysis, or loss of muscular coordination needed to produce speech is called *dysarthria*, a medical entity that differs from aphasia. This limitation affects the way speech sounds are produced, creating a range of deficits from mild slurring to the complete inability to produce sounds.

This case history, told by a speech-language pathologist, is an example of a highly specific and rather complex type of aphasia that primarily involves the production of language. As you read it, imagine the frustration of someone who knows what they wish to say, but cannot express the thoughts as others normally do.

Mr. S. could comprehend speech when you conversed with him in simple words and sentences.

But, when the concepts became complex, either in the number of elements in the sentence or in its level of abstraction, he would become confused.

His output or production of language, however, was extremely impaired. When I first met him he was about six weeks poststroke. His spontaneous speech was limited to no more than a few words at a time and he struggled to get those words out. He could not speak in complete sentences or put sentences together to make a story. He seemed to know what he wanted to say, but could not get the words out.

To make his needs known he would try to speak in short phrases. If I asked him whether he liked his new shirt, for instance, he might only be able to say, "not fitting." He could also point to objects and sometimes make appropriate gestures to help get his ideas across.

He also encountered difficulty naming familiar objects like *desk, pencil,* or *chair.* It wasn't that he didn't understand what they were, but he could not produce their names. It was as though his brain was a computer and he could not get the right words out of the machine.

Although Mr. S. had been a successful accountant, he could not write numbers past *five.* And, he was limited in his ability to spell words past the primer-level, like *go, run,* or *top.* All of this was quite frustrating and perplexing to him, since he had been used to carrying out complicated calculations and communicating complex ideas in his everyday activities.

The type of deficit illustrated here is called a *Broca's nonfluent aphasia,* named after Pierre Paul Broca (1824–80) the French physician who performed early studies to map the control centers of the human brain. Through performing a postmortem autopsy on a patient who had suffered left frontal lobe damage, Broca identified the correlation between language deficits and specific areas of cerebral injury (see also chapter 2). From Broca's work, and from the dilligent efforts of others, medical science has been able to map out many of the brain's language centers.

In a Broca's aphasia, like the one described with Mr. S., the ability to understand (receive) communication is largely preserved. But, the ability to produce language (speak, write, and make useful gestures) is more severely impaired. This type of deficit creates a "word-by-word" speaker, who can only utter single words or short phrases at one time.

On the other hand, there are individuals who exhibit deficits in their ability to receive communication. The following example, also told by a speech pathologist, describes a disorder primarily affecting the ability to comprehend language:

> Mrs. J. suffered a type of aphasia called *Wernicke's aphasia,* named after Dr. Karl Wernicke (1848–1905) the famous German neurologist. His work with the human brain revealed that there was a separate region devoted primarily to the *understanding* of language: reading, listening to speech, and understanding gestures. These are all *receptive* language functions and deficits in comprehension may be described as receptive aphasia.
>
> Mrs. J. had suffered a stroke that had affected her left temporal lobe. This is the area of the brain behind the frontal lobe—roughly in back of the ear. Her comprehension of spoken language was spotty and intermittent. She would often hear a word, but not understand its meaning or significance. If I would ask her, "Where is the telephone?" she might point to the chair.
>
> Because of this she would be inconsistent in answering even simple yes and no questions. Sometimes it was difficult for the medical staff and her family to know what she needed. She could not, for instance, reliably point to body parts such as the chin, elbow, or foot. When I would ask her to follow directions, she made many mistakes. She could function best, if there was only one critical element in the command, such as "Open the book." If I asked, "Open the book and put it on the desk," she would be unable to perform the activity.

What is striking about Mrs. J. and some other individuals who share this problem, is that she could speak rather *fluently*. Her spontaneous speech sounded normal until you listened carefully to its component parts and attempted to decipher its meaning. She might use well-formed sentences, but then intersperse them with phrases that to the critical listener had no meaning whatsoever. The melody of her voice was also usually appropriate, but again the meaning was usually unintelligible.

One of the characteristics of this type of aphasia is the use of *neologisms* or nonsense words. These are words like *blar* and *rab* that have no communicative function. They are made up in the mind of the aphasic. I knew that she used these words because of her stroke. In some situations, however, people are unfairly thought of as confused, disoriented, or even mentally ill, because they use nonsense words. But, this is the result of their specific type of cerebral injury.

Mrs. J.'s aphasia is one of the many types of language and speech disorders encountered after a cerebrovascular accident. Communicating is a highly complex and specialized activity of the human brain that has developed over millions of years of evolution. This development has meant that highly specialized discrete areas control different language activities. Because an individual stroke may affect one or many areas, or may involve minor or a significant total area of injury, there is the potential for a variety of resulting communicative problems. It is possible, for instance, for an individual to be able to sing, but to barely be capable of speaking intelligible thoughts.

An extremely disturbing problem is that individuals may at times seem to communicate with facility and at other times be confused, inappropriate, or even bizarre. They may, for example, break down into a repertoire of primitive language or curses. As we shall discuss later, it is known that fatigue, a variety of emotional states, and the presence of conflicting stimuli may adversely affect communication. Anyone who has felt tongue-tied or suddenly nervous in a new or frightening situation (such as public speaking or traveling in a foreign country) has experienced this situation firsthand. For the person with aphasia, the tendency to be confused or inappropriate in the face of simple distractions is greater. This includes commonplace social situations like trying to talk at a party where there is music or on a busy street. The lack of predictability about the ability to communicate can be terribly trying for people with aphasia.

In spite of the complexity of language and its dependence upon emotional and motivational factors, there are significant gains that can be made through intensive speech and language rehabilitation. The improvements made in this area are particularly rewarding because language is so important—to our sense of self-worth, ability to relate to others, and independence. Without communication we are inevitably left alone, remote, confused, and hindered in every aspect of daily living.

## Symptoms of Aphasia

From the preceding discussion, it should be clear that there are many different types of aphasia. Moreover, the *extent* of any individual's deficit will depend on the severity of cerebral injury and will be compounded by many social and environmental factors. Thus, an aphasia may be mild, moderate, or severe, but within each level there may be times when communicating is relatively easy or extremely impaired. For our purposes of explanation, we will divide the general subject into two broad categories: *receptive impairments* (listening) and *expressive impairments* (speaking). These descriptions do not, in all respects, correspond to the terms and categories used by medical professionals, but they will help us understand the problem as it affects people who have had a stroke. If you use these terms with your medical providers, you will be able to communicate with them about aphasia.

### Receptive Impairments

Receptive impairments involve a loss of part or all of the capability to understand language and communication. After a stroke, most individuals with these deficits will be capable of some level of comprehension. Only rarely is an individual deprived of all functioning, unless they are in deep coma.

For our purposes three different types of deficit exist. Individuals may be impaired on the *one-word level,* in the ability to understand language because of its length or *grammatical* construction, or due to difficulties in the comprehension of *abstract* or *conceptual ideas.*

On the one-word level the individual may not understand the specific word that is being communicated, even though hearing is intact. Any sentence that uses the involved word may seem confusing or unintelligible.

This individual may be helped by the use of verbal cues and gestures. When trying to explain the word *comb,* for instance, nonverbal cues like performing a combing motion with your arm may improve comprehension.

As with all receptive disorders, the one-word impairment is often unpredictable and intermittent. A relatively simple word may not be understood, while a seemingly more complex one is fully comprehended. Or, the same word may be understood at one moment and not at the next. It may be appropriately received when used in a simple sentence, but unintelligible when part of a complex phrase or sentence.

Speech and language may become unintelligible because of the *grammatical* construction. In this case the order and placement of the words becomes the problem, even though the individual words may be understood. In effect, it is the way in which the words are *put together* that creates difficulty.

Sometimes it is merely the order that presents the problem. "The man was bitten by the dog," is an example of a typically confusing sentence. If the same concept is presented as, "The dog bit the man," comprehension is more likely. Stated in the first way, the individual with receptive impairment may be confused as to who does the biting and who is bitten.

On other occasions the sentence may contain too many words or choices. Thus, "Do you want coffee or tea?" may be poorly understood. "Do you want coffee?" followed by "Do you want tea?" however, may be readily appreciated. In communicating with individuals who suffer from receptive difficulties, it is often helpful to keep sentences short and simple and to reduce commands or questions to a single idea or subject.

A third general category of receptive impairment results from the difficulty in understanding *abstractions* and *concepts*. Each individual word in a sentence may be understood, but the overall idea is not comprehended. A question like, "Will a stone sink in the water?" may produce this type of deficit. Understanding here involves not only knowing what both stone and water are, but puts them together with the more abstract and implied notion of density.

Receptive impairments may also involve deficits in understanding gestures and in reading. Comprehending the written word is often more difficult than understanding speech in the aftermath of a stroke. That may be, in part, because conversation provides helpful cues like facial expression, pointing to objects, "acting out" situations, and the tone of one's voice. In communicating with an individual with aphasia, it is helpful to be creative and to recruit many nonverbal cues to the conversation.

## Expressive Impairments

Expressive impairments involve a loss of part or all of the ability to produce communication. These disorders, like receptive problems, may be mild, moderate, or severe; and may be intermittent and somewhat unpredictable. Communicating with others often involves a variety of activities: use of body language and gestures and pointing, and changing voice inflection and tone. Humans are also unique in that they can write, use the telephone, communicate through music, and perform other *complex* communicative activities.

A basic impairment of the expressive type involves difficulty with *word-finding;* a deficit in the ability to express the desired and appropriate word. Under this category we can include *paraphasia*, the substitution, omission, addition, or transposition of whole words or parts of words; and neologism, the fabrication of words or sounds that are not part of our language.

An example of a paraphasia is *pheletone* when the desired word is *telephone*. In this case there has been the transposition of the sounds and syllables. The use of *tomb* for *comb* is an example of a substitution paraphasia in which the *t* has been substituted for the *kuh* sound. Some paraphasias are confusing because the added, deleted, or otherwise changed sound creates a real word; for instance, *bred* used instead of *bed*.

Neologisms are made up words that have no meaning or that do not exist in our language. Mrs. J., in our last example, used many neologisms as a result of her expressive disorder. This is often characteristic of a serious type of speech and language dysfunction in which there are also a variety of severe comprehension problems.

*Agrammatism* is a second type of expressive symptom. Appropriate words are used, but only with extreme limitation of their organization into phrases, sentences, and the commonplace units of communication. In this situation it is typical that the individual is limited to short expressions like *not now* or *want water*. Full sentences, even extremely short ones, may be lacking. A less severe form of this disorder would include the formulation of simple sentences, but not complex sentences, paragraphs, or complete stories.

*Fluent aphasia* is the somewhat uncommon, but often startling problem exhibited by Mrs. J. In this situation intelligible words may be spoken in rapid fire, but their meaning and organization is garbled. Sometimes real words are mixed with neologisms and paraphasias.

Characteristic of this type of aphasia is the absence of vital words, at least for short periods of time. When this occurs, not a single word in an entire utterance will have communicative value. While the inflection may be normal and the effect appropriate, the overall effect is unintelligible.

Writing is, perhaps, the most difficult and complex of human language skills. Anyone who has studied a foreign language knows that both speaking and reading are usually much easier than writing. As children we may learn to speak with facility by late infancy and to read in early grade school. Sophistication in writing, however, takes far longer. It is not surprising, therefore, that after a stroke, retraining in writing skills may be a slow and laborious process.

At the very extreme of the aphasia continuum is a *global* disorder. This refers to an almost complete loss of language function.

Many, if not most, individuals who suffer a stroke have some component of both receptive and expressive impairment.

Rehabilitation, therefore, generally involves improving both receptive and expressive language skills. The speech therapist is trained to provide these services in an integrated manner, so that the ultimate goal is to improve the overall ability to communicate with others.

# Aphasia and Intelligence

Communicating with others is one of the principal ways in which humans demonstrate intelligence. We do this through the explanation of ideas, computation, and verbal fluency—in fact—in virtually every way in which we interrelate with others. While individuals with aphasia have speech and language deficits, they do not have an actual dimunition of their intelligence. A stroke does *not*, in general, affect intelligence.

Furthermore, the primary impact of aphasia is on the processing of language, not on the function of memory. Thus, individuals with uncomplicated aphasia know who their loved ones are, recognize their physician, and generally remember as others do, even though they may be inappropriate in their naming of people. Except for a few persons with aphasia who suffer multiple strokes, most individuals with language deficits do not have dementia (senility).

Nevertheless, the presence of communicating difficulties does alter mental functioning over the long run. Our mind, like our muscles, exhibits a "use it or lose it" pattern. If we withdraw from communicating with others, it is likely that overall mental functioning will decline over time. This is probably not a loss of intelligence, as we usually think of it, but the result of not using the brain to perform complex tasks. Unfortunately, this is often a significant problem for individuals with aphasia. As they withdraw from the social and intellectually stimulating world, they develop increasing difficulties in carrying out the mental activities that are necessary for useful and effective participation in society. In addition, the lack of confidence that customarily occurs in this context, further aggravates the person with aphasia and reinforces feelings of inadequacy.

Stimulation and interaction with others is the most effective method for overcoming this vicious circle of events. Combined with professional speech and language rehabilitation, the ultimate goal is to retrain these people to become active in the family, community, and workplace.

## Helpful Hints

While individuals with aphasia suffer from a range of language problems, there are some general strategies that will help most to facilitate communication. Read the suggestions that follow and adapt them to the specific needs of the person you know.

Also, you should work with the speech-language pathologist who is providing rehabilitative services. Learn about the specific deficits and needs of the individual you wish to communicate with. The supervising physician and other members of the stroke unit team may also be helpful in this regard.

One general comment that applies to all persons with speech and language impairment is to *avoid infantilizing* them. Talking to an individual with aphasia is not like talking to an infant. A stroke does not, in general, diminish intelligence. The person who has suffered a cerebrovascular accident is usually extremely upset about their illness and conscious of their impairment in communication.

1. Whenever possible, keep communication simple. Construct sentences in a basic subject-verb-object format and avoid unnecessarily long or abstract constructions.
2. Speak slowly and enunciate each word clearly. Avoid having your words run together.
3. Position yourself so that your face and body can be seen. Use appropriate and slightly exaggerated hand gestures, vocal tone, and inflection to further explain your thoughts.
4. When possible, use pictures to clarify your ideas.
5. Be alert to the presence of other handicaps like visual or auditory deficits and take appropriate measures to make yourself clear.
6. Avoid communicating in the face of distractions. Block out extraneous noise or stimuli. Street

scenes and parties, for example, are often particularly difficult social situations.

7. Be alert to fatigue or lack of attention on the part of the person with aphasia. In addition, lack of motivation will further limit efforts at communication. Choose a time to relate when there is likely to be the best chance of success.

8. Be mindful that the telephone is often particularly difficult for individuals with aphasia. Speak clearly, using simple words, phrases, and sentences.

9. Take more time in new and unusual situations.

10. Be patient in the face of slow word retrieval, incorrect word choices, or other manifestations of aphasia. Individuals who have communicative deficits are often extremely sensitive to their problem. Be patient, courteous, and cooperative.

11. Be encouraging. There is a tendency for individuals with language impairment to shrink away from communicating because they feel embarrassed. Be aware that shying away from communicating will create added future difficulties. Getting out of practice in the use of language produces the "use syndrome" and social isolation.

13. Use singing, reading aloud, and records to practice communication.

# Nonvocal Communication

A variety of nonverbal techniques have been developed to assist communication for individuals with dysarthria (see chapter 2). For these people receptive and expressive language functions are largely intact, but the ability to speak intelligible words is impaired due to deficits in the coordination of the vocal cords, tongue, soft palate, lips, and mouth.

Dysarthric persons must overcome problems that affect the voice quality, including its loudness, pitch, clarity, rhythm, rate, and melody. The techniques for retraining involve slowing the rate of speech, performing oral-motor exercises to strengthen and improve coordination, improving the posture important for speech production, and the use of assistive devices for nonverbal communication.

There are numerous exercises that can be performed under the supervision and tutelage of the speech pathologist. Repetition of vowel sounds (*a,e,i,o*, and *u*) strengthen the vocal cords. The *k* and *g* sounds work on the soft palate and back of the tongue. The *p*, *b*, *m*, and *w* sounds improve lip strength and coordination. Exercises involving pursing and retracting the lips also improve strength. And, licking the lips all around in a circular motion, improve the range of motion of the tongue.

Other techniques involve the use of gestures. There are word and picture charts that can be made up for the individual's needs and interests. They can point to the appropriate picture to get meaning across.

Another simple device is a grid of words and letters that can be individualized for the dysarthric person's communicative needs. He can keep one or more of these charts handy and point to each word (or series of letters) to produce the desired communication (see Table 1). By pointing to the appropriate boxes in sequence, it is possible to create a wide range of communicative phrases; for example, "I am hungry," or "He is angry." By using the letters in sequence it is possible to spell out words to communicate concepts not included in the words on the chart.

In recent years a number of electronic and computerized devices have been designed to help the nonspeaking individual. They are generally most helpful for individuals with motor disorders that impair speech, but may also assist some people with aphasia. The Cannon Communicator, for instance, is like a miniature typewriter that produces a printed message. The Vocaid electronically produces a spoken word or short phrase. In general, these devices are expensive. They should be purchased only after a full evaluation by a speech-language pathologist.

## Other Assistive Aids

Many devices have been developed that assist with the *physical* aspects of communicating. Training in the use of these is usually part of the work carried on by the occupational therapist. Since they help primarily with the area of communicating, they are included in this chapter.

By and large these devices do not provide assistance in the mental functions needed for communication. A push-button telephone, for instance, assists with dialing, but it is not a substitute for the ability to recall or find the phone number. A card-dialing telephone can provide some additional assistance, but again it does not fully substitute for the mental activity of choosing the appropriate number.

Consult with your speech-language pathologist and occupational therapist before purchasing any of the following devices. There are catalogs that list additional equipment that may also be helpful. And, before you actually buy any device, find out whether its cost can be covered by insurance (see chapter 10).

## Devices for the Telephone

1. Shoulder Rest. For the individual who can pick up the phone, but has difficulty holding it during the conversation
2. Telephone Arm. An extension that permanently holds the telephone at a convenient height
3. Dialing Stick. A tool that fits into the holes of the dial
4. Push-Button Telephone. Reduces the strength necessary for dialing
5. Automatic and Card-Dialing Phones. These devices contain a memory or number that may be keyed into a card that performs the dialing

## Devices for Typing

1. Electric Typewriter. Can be a helpful substitute for a pen and pencil when writing ability is impaired
2. Typing Stick. Can be used to type out letters using the hand or the mouth
3. Self-Correcting Ribbon. Facilitates clear communication with the typewriter

**SAMPLE CHART FOR NONVOCAL COMMUNICATION**

|  | THE | IS ARE | AT | TO |
|---|---|---|---|---|
| E | A | R | D | U |
| WHAT | I ME | MAN | WANT | URINAL |
| T | O | I | L | G |
| WHEN | YOU | WOMAN | FEEL | SHAVE |
| N | S | F | Y | X |
| WHY | HE | DOCTOR NURSE | SEE | SHOWER |
| H | C |  | P | J |
| WHERE | SHE | LOUISE | AM | CLOTHES |
| M | W | Q | O |  |
| B | Z | JOHN | GO WENT | HURT PAIN |
|  | THEY | BETTY | EAT |  |

4. Automatic Carriage Return. Facilitates typing when strength, coordination, and range of motion is limited

5. POSSUM Typewriter. Developed in England, allows for stroke victims to type through the use of a *pneumatic* (worked by air pressure) tube controlled by the mouth

## Devices for Writing

1. Built-Up Pens and Pencils. Facilitate writing when the pinch grip is weak or if coordination is impaired

2. Pen or Pencil Holder. Substitutes for the pinch grip needed to hold the pen or pencil

| <u>V</u> | | | | |
|---|---|---|---|---|
| HAPPY<br>**K** | HOME | IN | DAY | MONDAY<br>TUESDAY |
| SAD | BATHROOM | ON | NIGHT | WEDNESDAY<br>THURSDAY |
| ANGRY<br>TIRED | BEDROOM | UP | AFTERNOON | FRIDAY<br>SATURDAY |
| COLD<br>HUNGRY | KITCHEN | DOWN | EVENING | SUNDAY |
| HOT<br>THIRSTY | T.V.<br>RADIO | | MORNING | TODAY<br>TOMORROW<br>YESTERDAY |
| DRINK | SLEEP | 1<br>4<br>7 | 2<br>5<br>8 | 3<br>6<br>9   0 |

3. Cassette Tape Player. Allows the individual to send messages verbally, rather than by writing

## Devices for Reading

1. Book Rack. Holds the book overhead or on a table
2. Prism Glasses. Allow for reading while lying in bed *(supine)*
3. Page Turners. Devices that range from a thimble to a mouthstick that facilitate turning the pages of a book, newspaper, or magazine
4. Talking Books. Recordings of printed material supplied without charge to qualified individuals through the Library of Congress

# To Review

1. *Aphasia* is the medical term for the loss of language and speech functioning.

2. The speech-language pathologist, or speech therapist, provides retraining in the functions related to communication.

3. Two broad areas of language impairment may occur after a cerebrovascular accident. Receptive disorders involve difficulty with understanding speech, the written word, and gestures. Expressive problems produce impairment of speaking, writing, and producing appropriate gestures. Within each category there is a spectrum of impairment from mild to severe.

4. Extraneous inputs, new situations, and emotional stress may produce increased difficulty with otherwise simple communicative tasks.

5. Individuals with aphasia should not be considered demented (senile), emotionally disturbed, or mentally impaired. In general, the loss of language function does not diminish intelligence or memory.

6. It is essential that individuals with aphasia have a regular opportunity to communicate with others, otherwise their ability to communicate will become even more impaired.

7. There is an enormous psychological benefit derived from regaining the ability to communicate after a stroke. Intensive speech and language retraining should begin as soon after the stroke as it is medically possible. Gains made in this area of rehabilitation will improve results obtained from other aspects of the rehab process.

8. Individuals with dysarthria have an impairment of their ability to produce understandable voice sounds. There are nonvocal techniques and assistive devices that can facilitate communication in the face of this deficit.

9. There are, in addition, assistive devices that help with the physical aspects of communication: writing, using the telephone, and reading. Consult with the occupational and speech therapists for the applicability of these devices to your situation.

# 9

# Coping with a Stroke

Just about every individual who suffers a serious illness faces difficult, often seemingly overwhelming, emotional adjustments to their disease or disability. While it is normal to feel sadness, loneliness, fear, anger, and other unpleasant emotions, it is essential that these feelings receive appropriate support and treatment. Prolonged psychological disability will inevitably produce disastrous effects on the rehabilitative process.

Fortunately, treatment for the emotional problems that arise after a stroke exists in the form of counseling, familial and community support, and medication. This type of multifaceted approach should be considered an integral part of the overall rehabilitation strategy. The professionals who can provide these services should be part of the stroke unit team. There is no way to avoid the fact that appropriate psychological therapy is as important as medical and nursing care; or physical, occupational, and speech therapy. In fact, it may be the foundation upon which all other rehabilitative efforts work.

Coping with a stroke may be somewhat different from adjusting to certain other illnesses because the underlying disease affects the brain itself. Scientific evidence suggests that profound and complex physiological and anatomical reactions occur within the brain after cerebral injuries. Thus, when we observe personality changes, or inappropriate behavior and emotions after a cerebrovascular accident, it is often difficult to know whether these effects are due to biochemical, circulatory, structural, or purely emotional factors. In all likelihood, many of these factors may interrelate to produce an array of poststroke psychological reactions. For this reason, coping involves the coordinated activities of different approaches: rehabilitative efforts, appropriate medical and nursing care, psychological counseling, behavioral and cognitive therapy, group interaction and support, and the supportive presence of loved ones.

# Coping with Illness

Through the work of Dr. Elizabeth Kubler-Ross and others, we have come to understand that most people go through certain common emotional stages when faced with serious illnesses. These feelings may also arise when we face other threats to our sense of self: illness or death of a loved one, loss of home or community, and displacement from the workplace. Illness is only one of life's many challenges, although it may be the most profound one.

It is common to feel angry. Often this means having the feeling of "Why me?" "Why did I have a stroke, while others continue to enjoy good health?" Individuals feel unfairly singled out by their disease. Healthy people feel a lust for life and sense deep injustice from the threat of death or disability.

Anger is, of course, appropriate in the adjustment to a cerebrovascular accident. It is normal to feel this emotion at any age. Individuals who are vigorous before the stroke—regardless of age—may feel anger at their sudden disability and possible dependence. It would be *ageist* (the term we use for prejudice based on age) to think that older persons who suffer illness blandly resign themselves to infirmity or to the notion that a stroke is a normal part of the aging process. In fact, as we shall discuss later, individuals who do not feel angry and frustrated over their disabilities are likely to be inappropriately depressed.

In the face of "Why me?" we nevertheless learn to appreciate the life that we do have. After a stroke the angry feelings can be harnessed to increase the effort at rehabilitation. For some people it may also be a signal to shift priorities away from the mad rush to work and succeed; and to take increased appreciation from personal relationships and the more spiritual aspects of life.

The problem with anger occurs when it becomes all-consuming. Angry persons push loved ones and professional care-givers away; often impeding the rehabilitation process. They often seem inappropriate and unmollifiable in their demands. It is important to understand where the angry feelings come from and to avoid getting *stuck* in this stage of adjustment. Inappropriate anger serves only to separate us from others who can be helpful, attentive, and intimate.

Along with angry feelings there may be a sense of *disbelief* or *denial*. As we have already discussed, denial may sometimes be a physiological sequel of a stroke. This is most commonly seen in persons who suffer injury to the right side of the brain, but may also occur in the face of left-sided damage. Some denial, however, is motivated by psychological factors and should be treated as an emotional disorder.

While denial is protective to a degree, getting stuck in this stage is potentially debilitating. The individual may fail to mount the required effort at rehabilitation; or may attempt to perform activities that are unsafe or beyond current capabilities. When denial is omnipresent, it may be difficult to make realistic plans for discharge, or to prepare needed alterations in the home that will insure safety and mobility, or to make the appropriate financial disposition of resources.

Denial may also arise within family and among the other loved ones. They may not accept that certain disabilities will be permanent. They may make inappropriate decisions in planning for discharge, or in making their own arrangements for carrying out the needs of their daily lives. They may also be inappropriate in their relationship with the person who has had a stroke—being incapable of accepting the physical reality and failing to deal with the resulting emotional and social problems that arise.

There may also be a period of *bargaining* in which many different second medical opinions are sought. While we have emphasized that every person who suffers a CVA deserves aggressive, professional, multidisciplinary efforts at rehabilitation, it is important to accept that there are limits to the existing knowledge and technology. There are no miracle cures or miracle medical centers. This bargaining is more common, perhaps, in cancer patients, but may occur after a stroke. Excessive bargaining is yet another form of denial.

*Depression,* or *anxiety mixed with depression,* are common reactions to any serious illness. Loved ones may share these feelings, as well. We will speak extensively about poststroke depression, since virtually all stroke victims will have this emotion to some degree. The point to make here is that it is normal to feel *sadness* and *loss* after a CVA. But, persistent depression becomes despair—the mortal enemy of life itself. Depression drives away loved ones and produces isolation. A vicious circle may ensue in which isolation creates more anxiety and depression. Depression is a potentially serious and debilitating disease with physical, as well as psychological, ramifications.

Lastly, according to Dr. Kubler-Ross and her colleagues, there is the stage of *acceptance.* This does not imply giving up, but means understanding the true nature of the problem and finding coping strategies to deal with its stresses. Acceptance does not necessarily mean the bliss often associated with a transcendental spiritual state. Even when one accepts illness or disability, it is normal to have all the emotions associated with daily living. There will be days and moments of anger, frustration, fear, sadness, and loneliness, as there will be times of pleasure and happiness. Life goes on, much as it does for anyone else. It is normal to feel all of the emotions that others do, even after attaining acceptance of one's illness or disability.

Often the emotions of anger, denial, depression, and acceptance run together. Few people go through life having their feelings progress from one neat and orderly stage to the next. There may be times when anger is mixed with denial, or times of denial and depression.

*The trap is getting stuck in any one of these stages,* and to refuse professional help. There are many professional and community groups available to help both the individual stroke sufferer and the family in making the necessary adjustments (see chapter 10). The professionals on the stroke unit and the supervising physician should also be resources for recognizing emotional problems and seeing that they receive appropriate treatment. No individual or family that has suffered a cerebrovascular accident should attempt to deal with its inevitable emotional stresses alone.

# Stroke: A Sudden and Catastrophic Event

As the term implies, a *stroke* is a sudden and often unsuspected event. The victim is literally changed in a swift moment, as though by a mere stroke of the hand. Individuals may be swept from good health to infirmity in a matter of minutes. The rapidity of the events is often demoralizing and overwhelming. Few people—perhaps no one, in fact—are prepared to deal with this type of change.

Take, for example, this story told by a psychiatrist who was asked to see a patient who had suffered a major stroke.

A few days ago I had the opportunity to see an eighty-year-old woman who had suffered a stroke. The event had occurred about two months before and both her family and physician were concerned that she seemed depressed.

When I went to the stroke unit to talk with her, I was struck by the fact that her demeanor did not seem depressed. When I came into the room, for instance, she was sitting in her wheelchair, awake and alert. She was well groomed, spoke to me freely, and smiled at times. She spoke of her illness as a catastrophe, but this seemed appropriate to me. She was, after all, still almost completely paralyzed on her left side.

I had been asked to see her, in part, because of her regular bouts of crying. It seemed that whenever she spoke of her daughter and grandchildren, her eyes would fill with tears. She would cry for thirty seconds, or a minute or two. The problem was fairly simple and straightforward. Her loved ones reminded her of her current dependency. She feared that going home to live with them would be a burden. She had always been active and a source of strength for the family and could not bear the thought of living as a burden.

My diagnosis was fairly simple. She was still overcome by the suddenness of the stroke. Her ups and downs and crying we call *emotional lability*—a common condition after a stroke. This was not massive depression, but a fairly usual reaction to a major change in life.

I think her family and physician, even the patient herself, were relieved to know that this was not a serious depression. They were pleased to know that this was not a second illness—despair— and that with time and support she would probably make the necessary adjustments.

An essential part of the treatment for the sadness and emotional lability after a stroke is the physical, occupational, and speech therapy provided by the stroke unit. Similarly, the nursing program that provides training in bowel and bladder control and other basic self-care activities, reinforces the concept that improvement toward regaining independence is possible. The strides that are made in the rehabilitation program enhance self-esteem and an appropriate reformulation of the concept of self that has been so swiftly damaged by the stroke.

It is also helpful to be clear and honest with the person about their mood swings. Relearning the appropriate expression of emotion is part of learning to cope with a stroke.

It is also important to remind the person who has had a stroke of the subtle gains he makes toward independence. After a stroke, regaining capabilities may be excrutiatingly slow and hence not appreciated. It is helpful to remind the stroke victim of little gains like, "When you began rehabilitation two weeks ago you couldn't wash yourself and now you can bathe your face and chest."

A third area of support and counseling occurs when the stroke victim is oriented toward the future. He gains emotional strength from preparing for next week's rehabilitative program, a short trip outside, or future social events.

The sudden nature of a stroke often produces feelings of *fear* and *uncertainty* about the future. During the initial days after the CVA physical and mental functioning may be severely impaired. At first the person may be in a coma or suffer from a markedly altered mental status. One side may be completely paralyzed. It may be impossible to control bowel or bladder function, or to take meals. In the face of these disabilities it is understandable to worry about the future.

Unfortunately, during the initial period after a stroke there is often no completely accurate way for medical caregivers to predict the amount of recovery that will take place. This is usually extremely unsettling for the stroke victim and his family. There is no alternative but to try to be optimistic and to be mindful of the smallest signs of progress. Uttering a few words, coordinating simple movements, and showing the will to live are hopeful signs. It is, nevertheless, necessary to accept that a period of fear and uncertainty is normal.

# Impulsive Behavior after a Stroke

Some individuals who suffer a cerebrovascular accident become markedly *impulsive* in their behavior and manner. They make rapid and uncontrolled movements, or attempt activities that they cannot perform safely. They may seem inappropriately irritable or hot tempered at times.

This impulsiveness is different from anxiety or emotional lability (unstableness) also noted after a stroke. It seems likely that it is due, at least in part, to physiological changes in the brain as a result of the cerebral injury. And, like the labile individual, the person may be unaware or baffled by his own impulsiveness.

Dealing with the extremely impulsive person is often quite difficult. He must be prevented from attempting activities that may be dangerous. He may seem rude and aggressive in his manner. His speech may be difficult to understand and his thought processes confused.

Treatment for this involves many of the same strategies already discussed. He should be reminded of the appropriate behavior during therapy sessions, carefully observed while attempting physical therapy and the activities of daily living, and counseled concerning appropriate behavior in social situations. Family members and friends should be aware that this is part of the illness and not necessarily a reflection of the individual's feelings toward others.

# Poststroke Depression

Some degree of depression commonly occurs after a stroke. This is more than sadness; it is an intense set of physical and psychological reactions to the illness. While the degree of depression varies, it is important to recognize its existence and to take appropriate steps to treat it.

The physical signs of depression are important clues to its presence. They include a loss of appetite, weight loss, lack of energy, easy fatigability, sleeplessness, pains that seem to lack a demonstrable physical cause, and constipation. Other physical symptoms may also arise. Anxiety may accompany depression, producing agitation, irritability, palpitations, sweats, and gastrointestinal complaints.

The psychological clues to depression are a lack of interest in others and the rehabilitation process, a gloomy feeling about the future, self-accusation, loneliness, fear, diminished self-esteem, and an overriding sense of pessimism. Changes may also occur in mental functioning producing slowed speech and thought processes, inappropriate periods of crying, or crying alternating with laughter, or times of extreme elation that do not correspond to reality. This is characteristic of the emotional lability already discussed, but appears in the extreme. Depression is a continuum in which the symptoms may be mild, moderate, or severe.

Mental functioning is often adversely affected in the depressed person. The simplest decisions may seem impossible to make. Attention span may be very limited. The individual may seem vague and removed from the world and even from its most immediate needs.

Poststroke depression is likely the result of a complex array of physiological and environmental forces. It is a disease process, not merely a self-limited reaction to stress, and should be treated as an illness. The following story is an example of poststroke depression, as described by a psychiatrist:

> I saw Mr. Green when he was about seven weeks removed from his stroke. He is a seventy-year-old, retired engineer whose stroke left his right side paralyzed.

As we began to talk, I noticed that his speech was very slow and that he had a lot of difficulty expressing himself. He seemed to understand me, but could barely speak.

He was also quite withdrawn and lifeless. When I first saw him he was sitting in a chair with his head and shoulders slumped over. He made no attempt to acknowledge my presence as I walked in the door and it took a lot of encouragement to get his attention.

Before going to visit him I learned from the nursing staff that he had lost weight and had little interest in eating or feeding himself. He looked frail and lifeless—not surprising for anyone who does not eat adequately.

The nurses told me, in addition, that he was often very irritable, particularly in the mornings. But, by mid-day he often fell asleep. He was not very interested in his therapy program and sometimes fell asleep during the sessions. He usually said that he didn't want to leave the stroke unit to go down for the rehabilitation sessions. It was as though he was disinterested in his own rehabilitation and had lost the will to regain independence.

After talking with him I learned that he felt overwhelmed by his difficulty in communicating with others. He had been born in Europe and before the stroke could speak six languages fairly fluently. You can imagine his sadness when he realized that he could not communicate. After all this had always been one of his strong points.

It was particularly ironic that he had been hospitalized in the United States. English was the last language that he had learned and his disability was greatest in that tongue. This is not all that uncommon after a stroke. People often lose the capability of performing the most recently acquired mental functions. He could, however, speak German rather fluently and was still functional in French. I conducted our interview in French.

My diagnosis was that he was depressed; not

merely sad, but actually depressed. Some of his depression was a reaction to his current language problem. Part of it, though, may have been due to actual brain damage that resulted from the stroke.

My treatment plan involved combining antidepressant medications with support and cognitive therapy. My experience, and the experience of others in the field, is that drugs plus counseling produce the best overall result. The two approaches together seem to be generally superior to either one alone in the treatment of depression after a stroke.

The cognitive therapy involves explaining the vicious circle of diminished self-esteem and psychological depression that often occurs after a stroke. I make it clear that each condition will feed upon the other. I also point out areas where progress toward independence is being made. I talk about the successes and make it clear that the situation is not hopeless.

Supportive therapy comes from the staff and from other patients on the stroke unit. Reinforcement is provided when gains are made and where there is a cohesive helping environment of staff and patients.

Sometimes the patient or the family ask me, "How long will it be necessary to take the antidepressant medicines?" There are no absolute or fixed guidelines. In general, once we start the drugs we give them for about six months. Near the end of the treatment period we begin a gradual process of reducing the dose and frequency of their administration. If all goes well we can eventually discontinue their use. It may be helpful, however, to continue with a program of counseling.

If, on the other hand, the person seems to be getting the symptoms of depression back while we are tapering off the medicines, or gradually eliminating them, it may be necessary to reinstate them at full dose. I then usually continue their use for about a year, before trying to reduce them again.

Mr. Green's appetite, outlook, and mental state improved with our approach. He became more motivated to participate in the rehabilitation program, improved his appetite, and was less irritable in the mornings. Like many who suffer a serious stroke, his depression was part of the illness that could not have been overlooked. I do not think that he would have been able to participate in the rehabilitative process without treating this aspect of his disease.

Many medical facilities are studying the treatment of poststroke depression. Different antidepressant drugs and other types of medical intervention are being tried. A variety of psychotherapeutic modalities are also being studied. No single type of antidepressant or form of therapy has been shown to be best for every stroke victim.

Some antidepressant drugs have markedly sedative effects, while others act as stimulants. Thus, the particular medication that is used should be matched to the individual's needs. Stimulating drugs may be most helpful in persons who appear lethargic, easily fatigued, or drowsy. Drugs that have sedating effects may prove more beneficial for individuals who are agitated, restless, or who have difficulty sleeping.

Antidepressants usually take a few weeks of continued administration before their full therapeutic effect is noted. They also require gradual elimination from the therapeutic regimen. They should not, in general, be abruptly discontinued.

These drugs also have a variety of potential side effects or adverse reactions associated with their use. They may produce abnormally low or high blood pressure, palpitations, or abnormal heart rhythms. Some also produce a dry mouth, blurred vision, nightmares, urinary retention, exacerbation or precipitation of glaucoma, constipation, anemia, and suppression of normal immune functioning.

There are a variety of potential adverse effects upon the nervous system including confusion, disorientation, agitation, incoordination, sensory disturbances, tremors, and drowsiness. They are, in general, incompatible with alcohol and potentially dangerous when taken with certain prescription and nonprescription drugs. A full list of all the potential side effects, adverse reactions, and drug interactions is beyond the scope of this book. If you are taking an antidepressant medication or know someone who is, learn about the possible reactions and interactions that might occur. If you have a question about their use or of an effect they are producing ask your medical provider. In other words, become informed and report any concern to your care-giver immediately. While most individuals who take these medicines do so without serious side effects, there are potentially dangerous adverse reactions and difficulties associated with their use.

## Coping with Change and Loss

A stroke is likely to produce intense feelings of *change* and *loss*. The loss of functional capacity, even if it is not severe, inevitably creates an alteration of self-image, changes in familial and community status, new financial problems, and often a different perspective on the future.

Certainly, a stroke is likely to feel like a brush with death, and to be an uncomfortable reminder of one's vulnerability and mortality. The potential for suffering another CVA may feel like a time bomb—an uncontrollable, possibly fatal circumstance. One strategy for coping with this is to employ relevant preventive measures (see chapter 4). Changing one's diet and life-style, starting an exercise program and taking prescription medicines are positive ways of adapting to this change.

It is also necessary to learn to cope with changes in physical functioning. A stroke is likely to produce sudden feelings of getting old and to exacerbate fears of losing mental and physical capability. We should remind ourselves that aging is a process that begins at birth and that our abilities are constantly changing. Only the very young do not face the daily need to adapt the ways in which they do things. Clearly this becomes a major factor in the face of partial paralysis, incontinence, or speech defects. But, the need for adaptability exists for everyone—regardless of age and health status.

We should also remember from Dr. Kubler-Ross that illness is only one of life's changes that demand adaption. We practice getting through the stages of coping in response to illness or death of a loved one, change of occupation or community, retirement, and divorce. A stroke is an extremely stressful event that demands flexibility and adaptation, but it is not the only difficult hurdle that must be overcome during one's lifetime.

# Social Isolation

The physical limitations, changes in mental functioning, and emotional problems combine to separate the stroke victim from his social environment. It is also commonplace for friends, even loved ones, to shrink away from the person who has had a CVA. Everyone begins to feel ill at ease. Again, this becomes a vicious circle. As the social options diminish, the ability to reenter society also suffers.

After a stroke even the simplest social activities like shopping, going for a walk, or using the telephone may seem impossible. For the person with language deficits, calling a friend or writing a letter may seem too difficult to manage. Individuals with physical limitations may be fearful of going outside the home or be unable to manage the automobile or public transportation. In the face of poor hand coordination or difficulty in managing meals, it may seem awkward to dine with others. Yet, these are the customary ways in which we relate to the world. Imagine trying to maintain relationships with others, if you could not use the telephone or share a meal.

Becoming self-conscious, and seeing oneself as some-how abnormal, becomes self-defeating. The more one feels under stress, the greater the likelihood of making additional errors of speech or comprehension. Or, take for example the athlete who has to perform under particularly stressful circumstances, like the baseball player who is at bat in the ninth inning with two outs and men on base. The same kinds of feelings arise when the person who has had a stroke appears in social settings. There is a nervousness about how well he will perform and a greater likelihood that the same nervousness will impair the result.

Many individuals feel acutely anxious about appearing in social situations in a wheelchair or with a cane. They may feel awkward about asking for help on the street or in public places. Unfortunately, many public places are still unsafe or inaccessible for individuals who are handicapped. For the person who has had a stroke this may be a new and potentially difficult hurdle in the attempt to regain one's social life.

The change in self-perception becomes all the more damaging by the reactions of others. In his autobiographical description of a stroke, Eric Hodgins pointed out that

> now something has happened to you, and you are somewhat different in ways both evident and subtle. Your old friend stands before you, unhappy and ill at ease; anxious to give no outward sign that he notices anything at all and inwardly wondering how best he can readjust himself to the somewhat different you he perceives.*

There are no easy answers to the problem of social isolation, but it is clear that it has negative effects on every aspect of the rehabilitation process. The longer the separation from society the more difficult the reentry. Psychological counseling and participation in group activities with others who share a similar problem can be beneficial. The American Heart Association and community agencies organize support groups and activities for individuals who have had a stroke or who suffer from other handicaps. If loneliness and isolation are issues in the recovery process, they should be treated as a part of the overall adjustment to the stroke illness.

# The Will to Live

The stories of Agnes DeMille, Patricia Neal, and others who have suffered strokes attest to the undeniable fact that the foundation for all rehabilitative efforts is the will to live. Without a lust for life it is unlikely that any individual will regain independence and health after a cerebrovascular accident.

It is difficult, if not impossible, to fully explain why some individuals have that lust, while others do not. Clearly, there are personal factors that exist prior to the stroke that impact on the emotions, health, and environment that is created afterward. There is also no way of minimizing the importance of the social network: family, friends, and community that can provide the support necessary to maintain the will to live in the face of a stroke.

*Episode* (New York: Simon and Schuster, 1963), p. 99.

Coping with illness is therefore based on a combination of factors: personal, familial, financial, and social. Taken together they form the basis upon which people struggle back in the aftermath of a stroke (see chapter 10).

# To Review

1. Virtually every individual who suffers a stroke can be expected to undergo periods of severe sadness, depression, anxiety, loneliness, and fear of death. Adjustment to these emotions may be impaired by physical injury to the brain sustained during the CVA.

2. A team approach involving psychiatric, social service, medical and nursing personnel working in concert produces the optimal means for treating emotional disorders related to a CVA. Left untreated, emotional problems will impair recovery and produce their own set of disabilities.

3. Most stroke sufferers can be expected to go through a series of stages in their adaptation to a CVA, including anger, denial, depression, and acceptance. It is helpful to bear in mind that emotions related to these stages are a normal part of the adjustment process.

4. Effective and intensive physical, occupational, and speech therapy produces important psychological effects; helping the individual overcome frustration and depression.

5. Antidepressant medications may be a useful adjunct to the treatment of poststroke depression. They are, however, not a substitute for the total rehabilitation effort of the stroke team.

6. A stroke removes individuals from their usual social environment. Efforts should be made to cope with this loss through family support, community and social activities, and occupational retraining. It is normal for stroke victims to feel uncertain about returning to social activities, but this process should be encouraged and supported.

7. Every effort should be made to encourage the stroke sufferer's *will to live*. This is the fundamental basis upon which all physical, emotional and social efforts at rehabilitation are based.

# 10

# Going Home: Services and Options

Before the rehabilitation program ends, it is important to begin to plan for discharge from the institutional setting. Almost always, the question arises: "Is it appropriate to return home?" This is often an extremely complicated problem. While most people who suffer a stroke wish to return home, it is sometimes not possible for them to do so.

Deciding on the best plan for discharge should include the advice and counseling of the stroke unit team. They are experienced in matching the needs of the family and patient to the available supportive resources in the community. They can also accurately assess the current deficits and give you an idea of how the situation may change over time. You will need to prepare for such diverse needs as cooking, feeding, shopping, doing house chores, engaging in social time with others, and making arrangements for medical care. It is helpful to know the extent of these needs before a final decision is made concerning living arrangements.

This chapter includes a list of questions to ask yourself when considering the decision to go home. It also provides a discussion of essential support services. Be aware that the availability of programs and services varies from community to community. Find out about the programs, professionals, and community services in your area before finalizing your discharge plans. Your local area office on aging is an important resource for this search, as is the stroke unit team and the Social Work Department of the rehabilitation facility. Other referral sources are also listed at the end of this chapter.

# Is Home Best?

Most individuals prefer to return home after illness or injury. Home is filled with the intimacy of loved ones, familiar sights, one's personal possessions, and the memories of a lifetime. But, when an individual is disabled, the physical, social, and emotional requirements of the home change suddenly. You must assess the limitations of home life, as well as its positive history, in making the decision whether to go home or to find another living situation.

The questions that follow can help organize your approach to this problem. They have been developed with the help of the Social Work Department at the Jewish Institute for Geriatric Care. Ask yourself these questions and discuss them with your medical care-givers. We suggest that you write the questions and answers on a sheet of paper. List the *pros* and *cons*. After you have written your answers and discussed the issues, set the paper aside and return to the decision in a few days. This will help to freshen your outlook. Then, in a family meeting that includes a skilled health care professional, reassess the issues and try to come to a decision that is appropriate. At this point, you will probably have a good idea of the best initial step to take in answering the question: "Going home?"

## Question 6. Are You Eligible for Government Entitlement Programs or Other Forms of Insurance to Cover the Cost of Home Care?

Make a thorough list of the ADLs like washing, feeding, toileting, and grooming (see chapter 7). Include limitations in language and communication that may be a problem. If there is difficulty communicating with others, for instance, will the person who has had a stroke be capable of calling for assistance in an emergency?

Use the input of your stroke unit team to help assess the areas of limitation and independence. Try to get an idea of which functions have reached a plateau and will hence require routine care. Add to this problem list any other medical conditions like heart or lung disease, diabetes, visual impairment, urinary dysfunction, *colostomy* (surgical formation of an artificial anus) care, and arthritis that may further complicate the ADLs.

Make a list of the medications and treatment that are needed on a routine basis. Assess whether you can provide these services yourself, or whether additional professional care will be needed on a long-term basis.

## Question 2. Do You Expect Additional Improvement In Function and Will This Require Additional Professional Services?

Add to your list those activities of daily living and medical conditions that may improve with additional therapy. Make a separate list of the professional services required in the home to make this improvement possible. Will occupational, physical, or recreational therapy be needed for this purpose? Will you be able to provide regular transportation to the rehabilitation facility or clinic to obtain these services? Would a nursing home or shared living arrangement provide helpful opportunities for socialization that might improve language and communication functions? If you are basing your decision to go home on the expectation of additional improvement in the ADL, consider the practicality of continuing the rehab program in the home.

## Question 3. What Are the Social and Emotional Needs of the Person Who Has Had the Stroke?

Find out whether the individual has a significant level of depression, emotional liability, of feelings of isolation or frustration. Discuss with a professional counselor whether there are situations in the home that are likely to produce anxiety, fear, sadness, or other troubling emotions on a regular basis. Assess whether the individual really knows where he is; that is, is he oriented to place, time, and person?

It may be that the expectation of going home is not fully shared by family and stroke victim.

Make a careful assessment of limitations in mental functioning. Is there a significant degree of confusion, memory impairment, or problems with cognition? Remember that appropriate mental functioning is important for personal safety and for the safety of the home.

## Question 4. Are There Relevant Health Problems in the Family Members Who Will Be Responsible for the Person Who Is Disabled?

Assess your own medical needs. Chronic illness like arthritis, heart and lung disease, and visual or auditory impairment, may undergo major stress in the face of the daily care of someone who has had a cerebrovascular accident. There is also added emotional stress associated with the care of a dependent loved one. Consult your own physician for advice in this matter.

## Question 5. What Are the Social and Economic Needs and Resources of the Family?

Be open about financial, occupational, and social requirements of the individuals who will be responsible for daily care. Even the best-intentioned family members and friends may become resentful if long-term changes in lifestyle result from the care of a disabled person.

## Question 6. Are You Eligible for Government Entitlement Programs or Other Forms of Insurance to Cover the Cost of Home Care?

There are a variety of government-sponsored programs that provide financial support and services in the aftermath of a disabling cerebrovascular accident. Long-term care in the home is expensive if medical, nursing, rehabilitative, and supportive services are needed on a long-term basis. Assess your ability to have the disabled live at home, in part, upon the availability of financial support from public and private programs. Learn about the eligibility requirements and benefits before you make your decision about taking on home care. There is a special section on eligibility for entitlement programs in this chapter.

## Question 7. What Are the Financial Resources of the Family?

Linked to your answer for Question 6 is the financial resources and needs of the entire family. Make a list of the expected expenses that your family will incur, which may be separate from the resources available to the disabled stroke victim.

## Question 8. What Community Support Services Are Available in Your Area?

If you think that you will need meals delivered at home, or medical and nursing services, find out whether you can get these supports in your community. Is there a physician who is willing to make house calls? Will your doctor take Medicaid or Medicare reimbursement? Are there appropriate security services and home-delivered meals? Is there recreation available through religious and social organizations? Is transportation available?

This is such a critical area that we have devoted most of this chapter to the relevant community services that may be required by individuals who are disabled by a stroke. Your local area office on aging, social worker assigned to the stroke unit team, and your medical provider are important resources for finding out about the services in your area. No two communities are exactly alike, so we cannot tell you exactly what is available within your area. But we have listed and described a full range of services that may be useful for the family and the stroke victim. Find out about these services before making your discharge plans.

## Question 9. Is the Physical Layout of Your Home Suitable?

Stairs, bathrooms, elevators, and the neighborhood, in general, should be evaluated. Will you need renovation to your home, such as grab bars in the bathroom (see chapter 7), an intercom system, handrails on the stairs, and adaptation of your kitchen to make the environment safe? Assess the total expected expense of these changes and find out whether some or all of these adaptations can be paid for by existing entitlement programs.

## Question 10. How Do the Family Members Feel about the Prospect of Having the Disabled Person Return Home?

This is often the most difficult question of all. Many family members may find it hard to express their reluctance about shouldering the burden of care. If the concerns are not dealt with before discharge, many unpleasant situations may arise that may ultimately be harmful for the overall recovery process. We advise that families discuss their feelings with a professional counselor who is knowledgeable about the problems that may arise in caring for an individual with physical, mental, and emotional limitations before deciding on the discharge plan.

The following story demonstrates how these factors can be assessed in the effort to make the most appropriate discharge decision. Be aware that there is no right or wrong decision for any individual situation. The important thing is to be clear about the needs of everyone concerned and to devise appropriate strategies that will insure a safe, happy, and positive discharge plan.

Janet was seventy-five years old when she suffered a stroke that left her left side impaired. As a result she was unable to walk independently and had difficulty with her speech. In spite of her limitations she was very motivated to return home and worked hard at the therapies that would help her to regain function.

Before her stroke she had been living alone in an apartment in a large city. She had been widowed for twenty years and her children had moved away. Although her children had been living far away, she was active in her local church and had many close friends in the neighborhood.

In formulating the discharge plan the stroke unit team had numerous discussions with Janet and her children. They also met with the minister of her church and discussed ways in which their services could be helpful.

When the time came to decide on going home there was a conflict of views. She wanted to go home to her apartment, but her children felt that it was not safe. They worried that the neighborhood would be a problem and were concerned that the apartment could not be adapted to her disability. When we were considering her needs, she was still unable to walk without a walker and she sometimes had difficulty with her speech.

We devised a two-step plan for discharge. Her first step was to go to live with her daughter. We arranged for regular visits from a nurse and coverage of other services under Medicare. Since she was planning on returning to her apartment, we encouraged her children to maintain the rent payments.

After two months she returned to her apartment. The minister made arrangements for regular visits from church members. They pitched in to help her shop, clean, and provide transportation. We contacted a local physician who agreed to take her on as a patient. He monitored her condition and we arranged for regular visits with a home health aide. Janet was an active woman and spent most of her days enjoying church events. She plays bingo, organizes community services for others and makes regular day trips with the church.

There were some renovations to her home that we considered important for her safety. The scatter rugs were removed, night lights were placed around the apartment, and grab bars were placed next to the toilet and tub. A member of the church who was a retired carpenter oversaw the physical changes in the apartment and we had a visiting nurse come and make certain that the bathroom renovations were appropriate for her needs.

We continued to see that she was doing well. One of the members of the social work staff called her on a routine basis and we received reports from the visiting nurse. After a few months we learned that although she could get out and around with her walker, she was afraid of falling outside the home. She felt "funny" using the walker on the street. We suggested that she join a community support group to discuss the issue. Talking about her feelings helped and the group also arranged volunteers to escort her to certain activities. She was able to overcome her self-conscious feelings and also to make new friends through the support group.

In spite of the difficulties involved, going home was positive for Janet. She overcame her fears and negative self-image and reestablished herself as an important part of her church and community. She now functions independently and has improved her physical functions and language abilities. Her children were also relieved. They were concerned for her safety, but they were not anxious to have her come to live with them.

One last thing that we did was to help Janet apply for the appropriate entitlement programs that would help her pay her bills. She had already been receiving benefits under Medicare, but like many individuals she was not aware of other programs that could be helpful. We worked out reimbursement for certain assistive devices, application to the Food Stamp program, and for payment of the home maker. Without these programs and the monitoring by the visiting nurse, Janet and her family would have had severe financial hardships associated with her living at home.

It is important to remember that going home is appropriate only when the many factors related to the individual, family, and community can be supported with appropriate services. There are, as shall be explained in this chapter, other options. Every individual and family must decide on what is best for their particular situation. What worked for Janet and her children may not be best for others. The rest of this chapter describes the support services that may be helpful for returning home and alternative living arrangements that may be appropriate when the home is no longer considered a viable option.

## Supportive Services for the Home

There are a variety of professional services, social programs, and volunteers who can help disabled individuals return to home life after a stroke. While no single individual or family will probably require all of the services discussed in this chapter, the list provides an idea of the complete range of supports that may be employed.

As was previously mentioned, there is no guarantee that your community will have all of these support services and programs available for your use. Your local area office on aging can be an essential reference for finding these services. You can locate this agency through your telephone directory or through your *state* office on aging. A list of all fifty state offices is provided at the end of this chapter. The social work department or discharge planner of your rehabilitation facility or hospital is also a useful referral source. They should be involved in the discharge planning and in making arrangements for community social services.

In general, we advise that you begin to make your plans well ahead of the expected date of discharge. It often takes time to apply and be accepted into entitlement programs, to arrange for renovations to the home, visits from health care providers, and rehab therapists; and for other appropriate needs. The transition from institution to home life is often difficult, and should be buffered by appropriate planning. Table 2 provides a schematic representation of the support services that may be relevant to your needs.

**Table 2**

# Community Service Checklist

| Services at Home | Supervised Living Arrangements |
|---|---|
| Medical Care | |
| Nursing Care | Enriched Housing |
| Home Health Aide | Shared Housing |
| Physical Therapy | |
| Occupational Therapy | |
| Speech Therapy | |
| Medical Supplies and Equipment | |
| Personal Care Aide | **Institutional Care** |
| Housekeeper | Skilled Nursing Facility |
| Adult Day Care | Health-Related Facility |
| Case Management | Residential Care Facility |
| Checking Service | |
| Chore and Home Maintenance | |
| Counseling | |
| Home-Delivered Meals | |

## Medical Care

It is helpful to make arrangements for medical care in your community *prior* to leaving the hospital or rehabilitation facility. You may wish to find a physician who practices alone, in a group, or in a community health center. Many practice arrangements involve physician assistants and nurse practitioners who can be an important part of the health care team. Make certain that you can get to the office of your health care provider. If you want a provider who makes home visits, request this before agreeing to become part of their practice. There are professional groups that specialize in this service. They can be located through your local Yellow Pages or medical society.

Find out where your physician has hospital privileges and whether he will come to the emergency room if you are suddenly in need of medical services. In addition, discuss the issue of fees and payment before making a commitment to a particular practice. Some providers will not take Medicare or

Medicaid assignments and others ask for fees in addition to the reimbursement provided by these programs.

## Nursing Care

Skilled nursing may be provided by a nurse practitioner (a registered nurse with postgraduate training), a registered nurse (RN), or a licensed nurse practitioner (LPN). In general, the RN has more training than the LPN and fees for their services run higher.

The nurse may visit the home to determine needs, carry out treatments ordered by a physician, teach management of care, and explain the physician's orders. The skilled nurse may also administer medications and assist in the carrying out of special dietary regimens. She also helps provide support and guidance for the family and the individual who has had a stroke; and may make referrals to community agencies.

Payment for nursing services can be arranged by the family or through public agencies. It is relatively uncommon for private insurers to pay for long-term nursing care in the home. The cost of RNs, LPNs, and home health aides (explained in the next section) will be reimbursed by Medicare for a limited time period, if the plan is ordered by a physician. In most cases the services of the nurse must be supplied through a voluntary home health agency that is certified by Medicare and be appropriate under the *Medicare Guidelines*.

A nurse who makes home visits should act as a liaison between the disabled person and other involved health professionals. This means monitoring health status; reporting observations to the supervising physician, and being alert to changing physical, emotional, and social needs.

It may be confusing to know exactly what nursing services are, particularly in how they differ from services provided by physicians, physician assistants, and other members of the health care team. Nursing, like other disciplines within medicine, has undergone many redefinitions of its role. Some typical nursing services are as follows:

1. wound dressing
2. urinary *catheter* (a tubular device inserted into the body to permit injection or withdrawal

of fluids or to keep a passage open, in this instance to the bladder) care
3. application of salves
4. monitoring vital signs
5. help with colostomy care
6. *tracheostomy* (formation of an opening into the trachea through the neck to allow the passage of air)
7. administration of medicines
8. administration of injections
9. monitoring general health status

Skilled nurses do not, in general, make a medical diagnosis, order laboratory tests, or prescribe medical treatment. They are trained to carry out orders prescribed by a physician or a physician extender (physician assistant or nurse practitioner).

Nursing services can be paid for out-of-pocket and are provided by private agencies and by public health programs. They may then include functions not covered under the Medicare Guidelines, like cooking meals, shopping for food, or those services that have not been prescribed by a physician. Before hiring a nurse it may be helpful to read over the Guidelines, which you can obtain from your local Social Security Administration office, Visiting Nurses Association, rehabilitation center, or office on aging.

Private nursing can be quite expensive, particularly if required on a long-term basis. If you feel that you need such services, it may be wise to rethink the issue of going home after a stroke. Skilled nursing facilities (nursing homes) have been designed for the purpose of providing long-term nursing. They employ a group of nurses who are supervised and coordinated to provide optimal care at a reduced cost.

## Home Health Aide

The home health aide usually works under the supervision of a skilled nurse and may perform limited nursing functions. These services involve simple nursing procedures like taking vital signs (blood pressure, heart and breathing rate, and temperature) and applying dressings. They may also assist with therapeutic exercises and provide assistance with ADLs like bathing, dressing, toileting, and feeding. They can carry out certain light housekeeping chores like cooking, cleaning, and washing.

These services may be reimbursed by Medicare. They must be performed only for the handicapped individual. In other words, it is not appropriate for Medicare to reimburse cooking, cleaning, or washing for other members of the family. Consult the Medicare Guidelines or your area office on aging for more details about reimbursement.

You can pay a home health aide to provide services. In such a situation he may carry out duties not spelled out by Medicare, including certain duties for the family. This depends on the private arrangement that you have with the agency and with the aide. Their services are usually less costly than those provided by a skilled nurse.

## Physical, Occupational, and Speech Therapies

The scope and type of services provided by these licensed professionals have been discussed (see chapters 6–8). Briefly, the physical therapist (PT) works on a program of exercises, instructions, and massages to help restore physical function and alleviate pain. The occupational therapist (OT) provides a program of exercises and instruction aimed at restoring the ability to perform the activities of daily living (ADLs) like feeding, toileting, dressing, transferring, and bathing. The speech therapist (also called a speech pathologist or ST) specializes in training to improve communication skills.

Reimbursement under Medicare may be available when these services are provided in the home. In general, the individual must be *improving* his functional capabilities. There must be a defined goal and progress must be made toward meeting that goal. Reimbursement will usually *not* be provided, if the individual has reached a plateau and the sessions merely *maintain* him at that level. There are guidelines for reimbursement that may be obtained from Medicare through one of the agencies or institutions already mentioned.

You can, of course, hire these professionals on a private basis. The cost of these services varies from community to community. Sometimes it may be affordable to do this at home, even if it is prohibitive to have regular skilled nursing. PT, OT, and ST sessions may be needed only once or a few times a week. Between sessions family members or concerned friends can perform the exercises and instructions on a regular basis.

## Medical Supplies and Equipment

Current Medicare and Medicaid rules *may* cover needed medical supplies and equipment in the home; private insurers rarely pay for equipment or assistive devices needed on a long-term basis. The general rule for Medicare is that the equipment must have a *therapeutic purpose* and be *prescribed by a physician*. Aids that provide comfort, soothing, or convenience are usually not covered. Medicaid coverage differs and must be applied for and considered separately.

Some of the rules and regulations that apply to supplies and equipment, do not always meet the needs of the individual who has had a stroke (see chapter 7). Bathroom equipment like grab bars for the toilet and tub may be essential for safety and functional independence, but may not be covered for reimbursement under Medicare. Contact your local medical supply house for a full list of the equipment that is currently reimbursed. Many suppliers print free brochures that list the available equipment and make clear which will be paid for by existing entitlement programs.

If you plan on paying for equipment and supplies yourself, be certain to shop around. Prices and services vary greatly from different suppliers. In deciding on the acquisition of any piece of equipment, ask your supplier the following questions:

1. Will the supplier arrange for delivery and installation?
2. Is there a waiting period for delivery and installation?
3. Is there an additional cost for delivery and installation?
4. What is the cost of renting versus purchasing the item?
5. Can you rent with the option to buy? (Ask your medical provider how long they think you will need the item, before making the decision to buy or rent.)
6. Is the rental equipment sterilized?

7. Does the supplier provide maintenance and repair services? If so, is there an additional charge for this service?
8. Will defective equipment be replaced free-of-charge? If yes, for how long after purchase?
9. Is free equipment provided on loan while the device is being repaired or while Medicaid approval is pending?
10. What is the company's policy on exchange or upgrading of equipment at a later date?
11. Will the supplier buy back the equipment at a later date, if it is no longer needed?

We advise that you consult a physiatrist, physical, or occupational therapist or other member of the rehab team before deciding on any assistive device.

## Personal Care Aide

*Personal care aides* may be called by different names in different areas of the country. Sometimes they are referred to as *companions*, *nursing aides*, *nursing assistants*, or *home attendants*. They commonly provide the following services:

1. help with bathing (shower, tub, and bedbath)
2. feeding
3. dressing
4. toileting
5. care of the teeth and mouth
6. hair grooming
7. shaving
8. manicuring
9. assistance with transfers (for instance, bed to chair, and wheelchair to toilet)
10. assistance with following a prescribed regiment of medications (they do not generally give injections)

If the person who has had a stroke is *alone*, they may help to prepare and serve meals, do personal laundry, change linens, make the bed, dust, vacuum, clean the room, wash dishes, and do other light housekeeping tasks. If other support services are not available, they may assist with the payment of bills and perform certain essential errands.

Medicaid may pay for personal care aides, provided that the handicapped person meets eligibility requirements. Medicare does not cover the services of personal care aides since they provide custodial services and are not health care professionals. Some functions that personal aides paid for by Medicaid cannot do are performing services that require a skilled nurse and providing housekeeping services for other family members.

In general, the cost of hiring a personal care aide is less than hiring a skilled nurse. You can find the service through a variety of proprietary agencies listed in the Yellow Pages or through your local area office on aging. They are often listed under "Home Care," but may have other titles. When inquiring, be certain to list the exact services that you require. You may, in fact, do well with such a helper and pay less than you would for a nurse or home health aide. However, you need to find out whether the personal care aide is qualified to provide the services that you require.

## Housekeeper

Sometimes the individual who has had a stroke can manage his activities of daily living, but requires services for taking care of the home. In this situation, a *housekeeper* may be all that is needed to help the individual continue to live in his own home. That person will do the laundry, cooking, shopping, light maintenance, and cleaning. They will *not*, in general, provide health-related services for the handicapped.

Often, housekeeping is not needed on a daily basis, or for a full eight-hour day. While these services are not covered by Medicare, they may be reimbursed by Medicaid, or be found at a fairly reasonable cost. There may be persons in the community who wish to have a part-time job for a moderate wage. You should inquire through your local area office on aging, senior citizens center, religious and community groups, and schools, to find the person you need.

## Adult Day Care

Adult day care is a relatively new concept in rehabilitation and in the care of older persons, in general. It is designed to be an alternative to institutionalization. A variety of ongoing adult day care programs are being developed throughout the country. While the full analysis is still pending, it appears that these innovative programs can help certain handicapped and elderly individuals avoid institutionalization.

Services in these centers vary greatly by location, available funding, and staffing. They may be provided from 1 to 5 days a week, usually from 3 to 6 hours each day. It is rare for the program to provide services 7 days a week, although this may become available in the future if the concept seems successful.

Some adult day centers offer medical, nursing, and counseling services and therapeutic activities. Transportation and hot meals (usually luncheon) are also generally provided. It is necessary to check on the actual services and availability in your area, since the concept is still somewhat new. Unfortunately, some programs are limited to supervised recreation commonly found in senior centers.

Another new idea is *respite care,* designed to provide *relief for the care-givers.* This may mean temporary institutional care and supervision or care in the home for a few hours a day, a few days, or on some other basis. The concept allows the care-givers to be free of responsibility in order to carry on with their own daily, occupational, recreational, or familial needs. Respite care is designed to take care of the social, emotional, and economic needs of the care-givers so that the handicapped person may continue to stay home.

Families and individuals can create their own community based respite programs by sharing responsibilities with others in the same situation. In one type of approach a group of families will pool their resources to provide respite care for short periods on a regular basis. They may, on the other hand, decide to alternate, providing the care by themselves. Yet another option is to find an older person in the community who can take on respite care responsibilities. Contact your local religious, community, and senior citizens groups for more information about the respite concept.

## Case Management

Another relatively new concept is the *case manager:* a service professional (often a licensed social worker) who can organize and supervise the handicapped person's care plan. This may involve—

1. coordinating appropriate referrals to community medical, nursing, and rehabilitation professionals;
2. securing coverage under existing entitlement programs like Medicaid, Medicare, Supplemental Social Security (SSI), Food Stamps, energy assistance subsidies, and other disability programs;
3. helping family members organize a regular plan for supervision and relief, including respite care;
4. seeing that appropriate assistive aids and devices are placed in the home;
5. acting as a link between the handicapped person, family, health professionals, and social agencies.

The need for case management is an outgrowth of the confusion and complexity of existing bureaucracies and the medical system. Some family service associations like Catholic Charities and the Jewish American Services Association provide case management without charge. Look under "Social Service" in your Yellow Pages, or contact the office on aging to find the appropriate agency in your area. Some social workers are now providing this service on a private basis, often for a modest fee. Your local organization of licensed social workers may direct you to a knowledgeable case manager.

## Checking Services

After a stroke it is common for both the family and the affected individual to be fearful of a repeat episode, fall, or other untoward event. It may be particularly frightening to return home, because there is the omnipresent thought that something might happen while the person is alone. A variety of *checking services* are available that permit the recognition of an emergency.

1. Postal Alert ("Early Alert"). The U.S. Postal Service has established a program in which the mail carrier may identify possible emergencies. A

red sticker will be placed on the mailbox. If mail collects, the carrier will notify the appropriate referring agency or service. Call your local post office or area office on aging for details.

2. Telephone Reassurance. A community volunteer or social service employee will call the home at a prescribed time and on a daily basis to insure that participants are safe and well. If the individual is ill, or does not answer the call, appropriate measures are taken. This may involve having a neighbor, the police, rescue squad, or medical professional visit the home.

3. Personal Emergency Response System. The personal emergency response system involves a small electronic signaling device that can be worn on a regular basis. It may fit on the wrist, hang around the neck, or be readily available in some other way. Some of the devices can be worn while bathing. When help is needed, a signal is transmitted to a central switchboard. The operator answering the signal carries out a preplanned program for insuring an emergency response. This may mean signaling a family member, neighbor, rescue service, or medical professional. The service should operate twenty-four hours a day, seven days a week. A variety of private companies and agencies provide the service; the cost differs by locality. In some areas hospitals provide personal emergency response services.

## Chore and House Maintenance

Taking out the garbage, shoveling snow, fixing faucets, and repairing locks may be difficult for the person who has had a stroke. Many communities already have networks of volunteers who will do repairs at a modest cost or on a sliding scale of fees. Your local religious and community groups may be able to provide you with information about these services.

If such a program does not exist in your area, it may be wise to make appropriate arrangements before going home.

High school students, retirees, and service-oriented persons may be available to take care of chores for the handicapped. Make a list of needs that will arise on a daily, weekly, and intermittent basis. You may not need a regular housekeeper or personal aide, but will require some regular assistance.

## Counseling

The stresses associated with a stroke usually do not go away with discharge from the rehabilitation facility. Marital, familial, environment, and personal problems inevitably arise in response to the needs of daily living. Most communities have a variety of professionals (psychiatrists, psychologists, and social workers) who are skilled in providing counseling and support in the face of these problems. It is best to be aware of these issues and to seek help before a crisis erupts.

Many communities have mental health clinics, certified agencies, and multiservice centers that employ these professionals. Their services usually cost less than when provided on a private, fee-for-service basis. Private practitioners, however, may be willing to see clients on a sliding scale basis. In some situations, psychological counseling may be paid for in part, or whole, by existing entitlement programs.

## Home-Delivered Meals

"Meals on Wheels" and other programs providing home-delivered meals are available for handicapped individuals who have suffered a cerebrovascular accident. In some situations the service is provided free, while at other times there may be modest charge. The number of meals provided varies; certain programs operate seven days a week, while others do not. In addition, special diets may be available for persons with diabetes, or other individual requirements.

# Supervised Living Arrangements

Even with the services we have discussed, it may be unsafe, uncomfortable, or impossible to return home. Nevertheless, alternatives to a skilled nursing facility (nursing home) may exist. The residences include a variety of *supervised living arrangements* that provide differing supportive services.

Planning for residence in one of these living arrangements should begin well before discharge, since space may not be immediately available.

Two general types of supervised housing exist: *enriched housing* and *shared housing*. In general, they should not be relied upon for health monitoring or medical care. These residences provide differing levels of support and safety for the activities of daily living. Consult your local area office on aging and social service personnel in the rehabilitation facility for more information about services in your community.

## Enriched Housing

*Enriched housing*, also called *congregate housing*, is usually a group of studio or one-bedroom apartments with common kitchen and living room facilities. Congregate meals, laundry, light housekeeping, and *limited* assistance with bathing, dressing, and grooming may be provided.

The cost of enriched housing and accompanying living expenses may be covered by SSI. Many of these facilities are sponsored by local religious and community groups.

## Shared Housing

*Shared housing* programs match people in the community who have extra living space with others who need housing. Rent is paid on a regular basis. Individuals make their own arrangements concerning meals, chores, the use of common living space, and other shared aspects of life in the home.

In general, these arrangements do not provide formal assistance in the activities of daily living and health monitoring. They are most appropriate for individuals who are basically independent in ADLs, but who do not wish to live alone.

Local community groups, particularly religious organizations and those concerned with seniors, may maintain lists of persons who wish to share space in their home. They may also provide assistance with placement and moving.

# Institutional Care

Most people tend to include all residential care facilities under the term *nursing homes*, but distinctions must be made on the basis of the actual extent of services provided, ownership (profit versus nonprofit), and participation in federal and state reimbursement programs (Medicare and Medicaid). The most common classification of nursing homes is based on the type of services provided, or *level of care*. The skilled nursing facility (SNF or nursing home) provides the highest level of care including skilled nursing on a twenty-four-hour basis. Even within this classification some nursing homes will not take residents who may have complicated medical problems or require intensive care. An intermediate care facility (ICF) or health-related facility (HRF) provides basic health monitoring and custodial care, but cannot provide services required for some individuals. Find out about the facilities in your area prior to discharge and see whether they can provide the care you require.

## Skilled Nursing Facility

Nursing homes are required by individuals who need continuous medical and nursing care including health monitoring, supervision, administration of medicines and treatments, and assistance with ADL. They provide nursing care on a twenty-four-hour basis and, in most cases, some form of physician backup.

Over the last two decades the popular press has made the public aware of inadequacies that exist in some nursing homes. It is, therefore, essential that you know exactly what you are getting before agreeing on admission. We suggest that you visit the facility and interview the personnel before making your decision.

In addition, you may find it helpful to question senior citizen organizations in your area about the facility you are considering. Some groups prepare formal evaluations of nursing homes, while others can provide information based on personal experience.

## Health-Related Facility

These institutions, also called Intermediate Care Facilities, provide custodial care and health monitoring. They are usually appropriate for persons who need minimal assistance with ADLs. The resident, for example, may be wheelchair bound, but fairly independent in transferring, continent in bowel and bladder functions, and be capable of self-feeding.

This setting may be particularly helpful for persons who have basically recovered from their stroke, but who have other medical problems like diabetes, heart disease, and vascular disorders that require medication and monitoring. Before you decide on this level of care, discuss the medical needs of the person who has had a stroke with your health practitioner.

### Residential Care Home

A third type of long-term care facility that is not a nursing home is the *residential care home*. It may also be known as a *board and care home, boarding home*, or *adult home*. These facilities do not provide medical or nursing care and are not eligible for participation in Medicare or Medicaid programs. They customarily provide group living arrangements and some assistance with the activities of daily living like meal preparation, feeding, and bathing.

The homes are usually paid for by the individual resident. SSI (covered in the next section) may cover the cost of room and board and provide a monthly allowance for personal expenses. Check on eligibility requirements. These homes are usually licensed and monitored by public agencies within the state. Information about them can be obtained from your local office on aging.

## Entitlement Programs

A cerebrovascular accident is a sudden and potentially catastrophic social event. The stresses of the illness are often compounded by the financial needs of the disabled individual and the family. Even when residual deficits are minimal, there may be dramatic changes in earning capacity. When long-term supportive services are needed, the financial resources of the family may be inadequate or severely compromised. There are a number of entitlement programs that provide assistance for needy individuals and their families.

The full range of programs and services available to the public are extensive and cannot be covered in full detail in this book. You can get the relevant information from the discharge planner or social worker in the hospital or rehabilitation center, local office on aging, Social Security office, or case manager.

## Medicaid

While Medicare operates uniformly across the nation under federal guidelines, Medicaid is a joint federal and state program administered locally. The benefits and eligibility requirements differ from state to state, but the program is designed in all cases for the financially needy. There are requirements based on income and resources that one must meet before benefits can be received.

## Medicare

Medicare is based on age and disability and has no requirements concerning financial need. It is a federal program administered by local insurance carriers. The guidelines are the same, in theory, in all states. If you are disabled for a protracted period of time, you may also be eligible for Medicare even if you are under age sixty-five.

## Supplemental Security Income (SSI)

To be eligible for SSI a person must be sixty-five or older or blind or disabled and have limited income and resources. Persons may be eligible for SSI in addition to the benefits provided through Social Security programs such as food stamps and Medicare. It is worthwhile to apply for these benefits at the same time.

## Other Programs

Handicapped persons may also be eligible for food stamps, Home Energy Assistance (HEAP), and job training. Specific visual deficits and other sensory losses may be helped through programs for the visually impaired, hearing impaired, and other groups. *Support groups* of individuals who have had a stroke and their families are organized by local chapters of The American Heart Association.

This is the story of a woman who achieved independence by employing a variety of community services and entitlement

programs. She is a good example of how independenc
involves a great many social supports, as well as the involve
ment of concerned family and friends. It is now more than
year since she left the rehabilitation center and she continue
to live in her community.

Mrs. H. was seventy-three when she suffered a
stroke. Before her illness she had been living with
her brother who is a few years older than she. And
although they were very close to each other, he did
not feel that he could care for her after discharge.

From the time we admitted her to our institution,
we hoped that she would be discharged back to her
community. So, during the entire process of rehabilitation we worked on organizing the community services that could make that happen. At first we
considered a health-related facility, but she was
adamantly opposed to that concept. To her that
seemed like going from one institution to another.

Her husband had been dead for eighteen years,
and her brother felt that he was too infirm to
provide care, so we began to consider other family
members. After talking with the entire family unit,
her nephew (who was in his fifties) decided to let
her move in.

During the rehabilitation effort Mrs. H. learned
to be independent with the use of a wheelchair. But,
both she and her nephew were concerned that she
might be alone in the house and need emergency
assistance. We made arrangements for her to wear
an emergency calling device that she could activate
herself.

During the day, when her nephew was working,
Mrs. H. had the help of an aide who provided basic
home-related services. The helper would shop, cook,
clean, and generally take care of the simple tasks
related to home life. Once a week a nurse came by
to monitor her health status. In the afternoons she
was taken to a senior center where she enjoyed a
variety of activities.

One of the very important things we did for

her and her family was to coordinate some financial supports. She was covered by Medicaid, but she had not known that she was eligible for benefits. This is a common problem. Even though the program is designed to help the needy, there are persons in need who do not apply for benefits. One of our jobs is to help individuals like Mrs. H. receive benefits that are available under the existing laws.

After living with her nephew for four months, Mrs. H. fell and fractured her hip. She was able to signal for help with her emergency call device. At the hospital her hip was repaired by a surgeon and she once again went through an intensive rehabilitation program. Upon discharge she returned to her nephew's house and continues to live with him.

The point that we wish to make is that the decision to return home or find other living arrangements after a stroke is a complicated one. Making the best decision involves input from concerned family members and professionals who can provide guidance and coordinate needed social services. Successful adaptation to a stroke often requires financial help, as well. If you do not feel that you are receiving the services you require, find out about the assistance you can obtain in your community. There are a variety of living options available. A full recovery from a stroke involves attention to the social needs created by the illness, as well as intensive medical, physical, and psychological therapy.

# To Review

1. Begin discharge planning well before the rehabilitation program ends. Involve all important family members and seek professional guidance from the staff members on the stroke unit team.

2. Ask yourself the ten questions we have outlined when considering: "Is home best?" Going home at discharge is not always the best option.

3. If the decision to go home is made, organize the appropriate supportive devices that will insure a safe transition to the home. Medical, nursing, and rehabilitative care must be provided, and there should be supports provided for

taking care of personal needs and the home. Find out about the programs and services that are available in your community before discharge.

4. If you have not made arrangements for home care in the past, enlist the help of a case manager, local social service agency, discharge planner at the rehabilitation facility, and your medical providers. They will help you anticipate needs that may arise and aid you in finding financial assistance to pay for the services.

5. It may be necessary to modify the home environment or purchase assistive devices in order to insure safety and comfort in the home. You should get professional advice before purchasing any equipment.

6. It is not unusual to feel burdened by the responsibility of caring for a disabled person. Get help before the feelings seem overwhelming. Adult day care and a variety of respite programs are available for this purpose.

7. A variety of safety and emergency checking services are available. Find out about the Postal Alert program, telephone reassurance, and personal emergency response programs in your community.

8. In some instances it is not feasible for the individual who has suffered a stroke to return home. There are options besides the traditional nursing home including enriched housing and shared homes.

9. There are institutional alternatives to the nursing home for long-term care. Two relatively common ones are the health-related facility and the residential care home. They provide different levels of care and services. Choose one that fits the medical and social needs of the person who is disabled.

10. There is a range of quality and comprehensiveness in the nursing home field. Some may continue providing active rehabilitation services, while others provide little more than custodial care. Before you decide on a particular nursing facility, it may be worthwhile to visit the institution. Community groups in your area, particularly those that involve senior citizens, may evaluate the skilled nursing facilities in your area.

11. Learn about the entitlement and insurance programs under which you can receive benefits. Because eligibility and

benefits change frequently, it may be helpful to enlist the services of a social work professional or case manager in order to receive appropriate benefits.

12. Your local area office on aging is an important reference source for the programs and services that may be helpful to individuals who have had a stroke. You can contact your local office through the telephone directory or via the state office on aging.

# Appendix A

## The American Heart Association

The American Heart Association produces information about stroke, organizes local support groups, helps with referrals, and provides other important services. National office:

American Heart Association
National Center
7320 Greenville Ave.
Dallas, TX 75231

## Medicaid and Medicare Information

Medicaid/Medicare
Health Financing Admin.
Dept. of Health & Human Serv.
Washington, DC 20201
(202)245-0312

## Written Material

Medicaid/Medicare—Which Is Which (516E)
Consumer Info. Center
Pueblo Memorial Airport
Pueblo, CO 81009

Your Right to Question Your Hospital Insurance Claim
Consumer Info. Center
Pueblo Memorial Airport
Pueblo, CO 81009

# Other Medicaid/Medicare Material

available from
> Superintendent of Documents
> U.S. Govt. Printing Office
> Washington, DC 20402

> Medicare and Health Insurance for Older People
> NRTA-AARP
> 1909 K St., N.W.
> Washington, DC 20049

> *Your Medicare Handbook*—SSA 74–10050
> *A Brief Explanation of Medicare*—SSA10043
> *A Guide to Health Insurance for People with Medicare*—
HCFA 02110
> *Home Health Care Under Medicare*—SSA 80–1004
> *Medicare Coverage in a Skilled Nursing Facility*—SSA
79–10041
> *A Guide to Supplemental Security Income*—SSA–11015

## Questions about Energy

> Department of Energy
> (800)424-9245

## Home Energy Assistance (HEAP)

> (800)432-6217

# Appendix B

## State Agencies on the Aging

State Agencies on the Aging provide information about governmental and private agencies that offer assistance for the elderly.

*Alabama*
* Commission on Aging
2853 Fairlane Dr., Bldg. G, Suite 63
Montgomery, AL 36130
(205)832-6640

*Alaska*
Older Alaskans Commission
Dept. of Admin.
Pouch-C-MS-0209
Juneau, AK 99811
(907)465-3250

*Arizona*
Office on Aging & Adult Admin.
P.O. Box 6123
1400 W. Washington St.
Phoenix, AZ 85007
(602)255-4446

*Arkansas*
> Office of Aging & Adult Serv.
> 1428 Donaghery Bldg., Suite 1428
> 7th & Main St.
> Little Rock, AR 72201
> (501)371-2441

*California*
> Dept. on Aging Health & Welfare Agency
> 1020-19 St.
> Sacramento, CA 95183
> (916)322-5290

*Colorado*
> Dept. of Aging & Adult Serv.
> 1575 Sherman St.
> Denver, CO 80203
> (303)866-2586

*Connecticut*
> Dept. on Aging
> 80 Washington St., Rm. 312
> Hartford, CT 06115
> (203)566-3238

*Delaware*.
> Dept. of Health & Serv.
> Div. of Aging
> 1902 North Dupont Highway
> New Castle, DE 19720
> (302)421-6791

*District of Columbia*
> Office of Aging
> 1012-14 St., N.W., Suite 1106
> Washington, DC 20005
> (202)724-5822

*Florida*
>    Aging & Adult Serv.
>    Dept. of Health & Rehabilitative Serv.
>    1323 Winewood Blvd.
>    Tallahassee, FL 32301
>    (904)488-8922

*Georgia*
>    Office of Aging
>    Dept. of Human Resources
>    618 Ponce De Leon Ave., N.E.
>    Atlanta, GA 30308
>    (404)894-5333

*Hawaii*
>    Exec. Office on Aging
>    Office of the Governor
>    State of Hawaii
>    1149 Bethel St., Rm. 307
>    Honolulu, HI 96813
>    (808)548-2593

*Idaho*
>    Idaho Office on Aging
>    Statehouse, 114
>    Boise, ID 83720
>    (208)334-3833

*Illinois*
>    Illinois Dept. on Aging
>    421 E. Capitol Ave.
>    Springfield, IL 62706
>    (217)785-3356

*Indiana*
>    Indiana Dept. of Aging & Community Serv.
>    115 North Penn St., Suite 1350
>    Indianapolis, IN 46204
>    (317)232-7006

*Iowa*

 Iowa Commission on Aging
 415 W. 10 St.
 Jewett Bldg.
 Des Moines, IA 50319
 (515)281-5187

*Kansas*

 Kansas Dept. of Aging
 620 W. 10 St.
 Topeka, KS 66612
 (913)296-4986

*Kentucky*

 Kentucky Div. of Aging Serv.
 Bureau of Social Serv.
 275 E. Main St.
 Frankfort, KY 40601
 (502)564-6930

*Louisiana*

 Louisiana Office of Elderly Affairs
 P.O. Box 80371
 Capital Sta.
 Baton Rouge, LA 70890
 (504)924-1700

*Maine*

 Bureau of Maine's Elderly
 Dept. of Human Serv.
 State House Sta. 11
 Augusta, ME 04333
 (207)289-2561

*Maryland*

 Maryland Office on Aging
 State Office Bldg.
 301 W. Preston St.
 Baltimore, MD 21201
 (301)383-5064

*Massachusetts*
> Massachusetts Dept. of Elder Affairs
> 38 Chauncey St.
> Boston, MA 02111
> (617)727-7751

*Michigan*
> Michigan Office of Serv. to the Aging
> 300 E. Michigan
> P.O. Box 30026
> Lansing, MI 48909
> (517)373-8230

*Minnesota*
> Minnesota Board on Aging
> 204 Metro Square Bldg.
> Seventh & Robert St.
> St. Paul, MN 55101
> (612)296-3544

*Mississippi*
> Mississippi Council on Aging
> 301 Exec. Bldg.
> 802 North State St.
> Jackson, MS 39201
> (601)354-6690

*Missouri*
> Missouri Office of Aging
> Dept. of Social Serv.
> Broadway State Office Bldg.
> P.O. Box 570
> Jefferson City, MO 65101
> (314)751-3082

*Montana*
> Community Serv. Div.
> Dept. of Social & Rehabilitation Serv.
> P.O. Box 4210
> Helena, MO 590601
> (406)449-3865

*Nebraska*

Nebraska Dept. on Aging
P.O. Box 95044
301 Centennial Mall S.
Lincoln, NB 68509
(402)471-2306

*Nevada*

Div. of Aging Serv.
Dept. of Human Resources
505 E. King St., Rm. 600
Kinkead Bldg.
Carson City, NE 89710
(702)885-4210

*Hew Hampshire*

New Hampshire Council on the Aging
14 Depot St.
Concord, NH 03301
(603)271-1751

*New Jersey*

Dept. of Community Affairs
P.O. Box 2768
363 W. State St.
Trenton, NJ 08625
(609)292-4833

*New Mexico*

New Mexico State Agency on Aging
La Villa Rivera Bldg.
224 E. Palace Ave.
Santa Fe, NM 87501
(505)827-7640

*New York*

Office for the Aging Agency Bldg.
2 Empire State Plaza
Albany, NY 12223
(518)474-5731

*North Carolina*
>Division on Aging
>Dept. of Human Resources
>708 Hillsborough St., Suite 200
>Raleigh, NC 27603
>(919)733-3983

*Ohio*
>Ohio Commission on Aging
>50 W. Broad St., Ninth Fl.
>Columbus, OH 43215
>(614)466-5500

*Oklahoma*
>Special Unit on Aging
>Dept. of Human Serv.
>P.O. Box 25352
>Oklahoma City, OK 73125
>(405)521-2281

*Oregon*
>Senior Serv. Div.
>Human Resources Dept., Public Serv. Bldg., Rm. 313
>Salem, OR 97301
>(503)378-4728

*Pennsylvania*
>Pennsylvania Dept. of Aging
>Finance Bldg., Rm. 404
>Harrisburg, PA 17101
>(717)783-1550

*Rhode Island*
>Dept. of Elderly Affairs
>79 Washington St.
>Providence, RI 02903
>(401)277-2858

*South Carolina*

South Carolina Commission on Aging
915 Main St.
Columbia, SC 29201
(803)758-2576

*South Dakota*

Office of Adult Serv. & Aging
Division of Human Development
Dept. of Social Serv.
Richard F. Knelp Bldg.
Illinois St.
Pierre, SD 57501
(605)773-3656

*Tennessee*

Tennessee Commission on Aging
703 Tennessee Bldg.
535 Church St.
Nashville, TN 37219
(615)741-2056

*Texas*

Texas Dept. of Aging
P.O. Box 12786
Capital Sta.
Austin, TX 78794
(512)475-2717

*Utah*

Div. of Aging Serv.
150 W. North Temple, Rm. 326
Salt Lake City, UT 84103
(801)533-8422

*Vermont*

Vermont Office on the Aging
103 S. Main St.
Waterbury, VT 05676
(802)241-2400

*Virginia*
    Virginia Office on Aging
    830 E. Main St., Suite 950
    Richmond, VA 23219
    (804)786-7894

*Washington*
    Bureau of Aging & Adult Serv.
    Dept. of Social & Health Serv.
    Olympia, WA 98504
    (206)753-2602

*West Virginia*
    Commission on Aging
    State Capitol
    Charleston, W. VA 26303
    (304)348-3317

*Wisconsin*
    Dept. of Health & Social Serv.
    1 W. Wilson St., Rm. 686
    Madison, WI 53703
    (808)266-2536

*Wyoming*
    Commission on Aging
    Hathaway Bldg., Rm. 139
    Cheyenne, WY 82002
    (307)777-7986

# Index

189

## ABOUT THE AUTHORS

DR. CONN J. FOLEY is Medical Director of the Jewish Institute for Geriatric Care (JIGC) and Chief of Geriatric Medicine at the Long Island Jewish-Hillside Medical Center.

He graduated from the National University of Ireland in 1972 and has had extensive training in both internal medicine and geriatrics both in Ireland and the United States. He is board certified in internal medicine and is a diplomate of the Royal College of Physicians in Ireland (M.R.C.P.).

The Jewish Institute for Geriatric Care, a 527-bed rehabilitation facility, provides innovative and renowned health care services, through a team approach, to older patients. The patients, whose average age is 83, are provided with both inpatient and ambulatory care. The institution has a major role in teaching geriatric medicine to physicians and other health care professionals. Its significant research undertakings have highlighted the potential for success in rehabilitation of persons with advanced age.

H. F. PIZER, PA-C, is a medical writer and physician associate in Boston, Massachusetts. He has written seven other books on health and medicine, including *The New Birth Control Program*, *The Post Partum Book*, *Coping with a Miscarriage*, *Guide to the New Medicine*, *Over 55*, *Healthy and Alive*, and *The Aids Fact Book*. Mr. Pizer is past President of the Massachusetts Association of Physician Assistants and winner of the 1981 award in the trade category from the American Medical Writer's Association.

# How's Your Health?

Bantam publishes a line of informative books, written by top experts to help you toward a healthier and happier life.

# NEED MORE INFORMATION ON YOUR HEALTH AND NUTRITION?

Read the books that will lead you to
a happier and healthier life.

| | | | |
|---|---|---|---|
| ☐ | 23113 | THE REVOLUTIONARY 7-UNIT LOW FAT DIET  A. Eyton & J. Carper | $3.50 |
| ☐ | 24775 | UNDER THE INFLUENCE Milam & Ketcham | $3.95 |
| ☐ | 23148 | GETTING WELL AGAIN Simonton & Creighton | $3.95 |
| ☐ | 24246 | DIET AND CANCER  Kristin White | $3.50 |
| ☐ | 24775 | UNDER THE INFLUENCE Milam & Ketcham | $3.95 |
| ☐ | 24514 | THE JAMES COCO DIET James Coco & Marion Paone | $3.95 |
| ☐ | 23888 | ARTHRITIC'S COOKBOOK Dong & Bank | $3.50 |
| ☐ | 20925 | WHAT'S IN WHAT YOU EAT Will Eisner | $3.95 |
| ☐ | 34106 | MY BODY, MY HEALTH Stewart & Hatcher (A Large Format Book) | $11.95 |
| ☐ | 23335 | GH-3-WILL IT KEEP YOU YOUNG LONGER  H. Bailey | $3.95 |
| ☐ | 23827 | THE HERB BOOK  J. Lust | $4.95 |
| ☐ | 23767 | HOPE AND HELP FOR YOUR NERVES C. Weekes | $3.95 |
| ☐ | 23818 | PEACE FROM NERVOUS SUFFERING C. Weekes | $3.95 |
| ☐ | 24279 | SIMPLE, EFFECTIVE TREATMENT OF AGORAPHOBIA  C. Weekes | $3.95 |

**Prices and availability subject to change without notice.**